# THE SONG OF THE LAMB

ROBERT CARDINAL SARAH

*In conversation with Peter Carter*

# The Song of the Lamb

## *Sacred Music and the Heavenly Liturgy*

IGNATIUS PRESS SAN FRANCISCO

Scripture quotations are from the Revised Standard Version of the Bible—Second Catholic Edition (Ignatius Edition) copyright © 2006 National Council of the Churches of Christ in the United States of America. All rights reserved worldwide.

Excerpts from the English translation of the Catechism of the Catholic Church, Second Edition, © 1994, 1997, 2000 by Libreria Editrice Vaticana—United States Catholic Conference, Washington, D.C. All rights reserved.

Except where otherwise noted, translations of papal and council documents have been taken from the Vatican website.

Cover Art:
Hubert and Jan Van Eyck,
*Ghent Altarpiece* (detail), c. 1432,
St. Bavo's Cathedral, Ghent, Belgium;
Frederic Edwin Church,
*Jerusalem from the Mount of Olives* (detail), 1870,
Nelson–Atkins Museum of Art, Kansas City, Missouri

Cover design by Thomas Jacobi


ISBN 978-1-62164-828-4 (PB)
ISBN 978-1-64229-371-5 (eBook)
Library of Congress Control Number 2025937953
Printed in the United States of America ♾

# CONTENTS

# FOREWORD

by Malcolm Cardinal Ranjith
Archbishop of Colombo, Sri Lanka

"Since the eucharistic liturgy is essentially an *actio Dei* which draws us into Christ through the Holy Spirit, its basic structure is not something within our power to change, nor can it be held hostage by the latest trends."[1] These words of the post-synodal apostolic exhortation of Pope Benedict XVI *Sacramentum caritatis* do indeed indicate the core of the deeper meaning of all liturgical action. From the pages of the Old Testament, one can already touch that reality, especially through the Scriptural depiction of the ongoing liturgy in heaven, where God continues to be praised and worshiped by the angels and the heavenly hosts.

## *Heavenly Liturgy*

The Isaian pericope of the call of the prophet is placed in the context of an ongoing heavenly liturgy (Is 6:1–6). Isaiah sees the Lord sitting on a throne that is "high and lifted up". The seraphim accompany Him. The holiness and glory of the Lord are proclaimed by these heavenly beings. At the voice of the angels proclaiming the holiness of God, the doors of the heavenly assembly are shaken and the house

[1] Benedict XVI, post-synodal apostolic exhortation *Sacramentum caritatis* (The Sacrament of Charity) (February 22, 2007), no. 37.

is filled with smoke. The altar is mentioned, from which an angel then takes a burning coal with which he touches the mouth of Isaiah, who is purified and can take up his mission. The same liturgical context is seen in the book of Revelation, where Jesus the Lamb is shown to be the content of the new heavenly sacrifice. The book of Revelation is full of liturgical elements that are used to describe the scenes of the heavens in apocalyptic times. The perfect Temple of Ezekiel (see Ezek 40) seems to be reconstructed in this narrative (see Rev 21). The scene is deeply cultic. The adoration of the Lamb is mentioned through hymns and canticles. Then there is the white-robed army of the elect who announce their faith in the Lamb (see 7:9–10), and one sees the descent of the Church, the new Jerusalem, from heaven (see 1:2, 10) with the seven golden lampstands and the long white robe of the Son of Man (see 1:12–13), the white garments of the elders and the saints (see 4:4), and the altar and the "amens" and "alleluias", as well as the expressions of praise and thanksgiving and all the prostrations, portraying a liturgical setting. What constantly happens in the high heavens is the bowing down, praise, and worship rendered to God the almighty by the elect.

Even in the formation of the Pentateuchal history and traditions, what emerges is that the codification of salvation history is closely linked to the worship forms of the Old Testament. The Credo formulas recited at the presentation of the first fruits in the Temple become the contour for the formulation of Israel's history. These Credo formulas are found in Deuteronomy 6:20–25 and 26:1–11.

The constant praise of God in heaven is the key to understanding salvation history as part of God's action to render sacred all of creation, freed from sin and transformed from its fallen state with the emergence of the new People of God and the New Jerusalem. Thus, worship of God is seen as nothing other than our own participation in the celebration of the heavenly sacrifice of the eternal Lamb and our association with that salvific *actio Dei* in heaven, which continues to transform earth and all its people into a state of holiness, to which it must all return. Liturgy, then, is not simply a horizontal effort on our part but our participation in that which is divine and very much the enactment of salvation in heaven. It is not made by us; it is given to us. We are invited to join the eternal sacrifice of Christ.

Besides, liturgy is the font from which our faith, or the *lex orandi*, emerges, along with the resultant *lex credendi*. The deeper we delve into it, the more intense our experience of faith in Him becomes. It then calls for a commitment on our part to a congruent spirit of moral transformation. It gives us the "power to comprehend with all the saints what is the breadth and length and height and depth, and to know the love of Christ which surpasses knowledge, that [we] may be filled with all the fulness of God" (Eph 3:18–19).

It is in this light that the sublimity of divine worship as *actio Dei* or *actio Christi* and our intimate and full participation in it should always be posited as a *sine qua non* for any meaningful and transformative experience of salvation. And so, there is a certain "givenness" in liturgy such that we are not necessarily its "creators" but participators, unworthy though we may be. Our task is to recognize the immensity of what is already happening in the presence of God, be respectful of what we have received, faithfully adhere to this *actio Dei* of heavenly and sanctifying praise, and make our lives compatible with these mysteries.

Our devout and fruitful participation in the heavenly liturgy will continue to challenge us to a transformation of our lives and our divinization until God will be "everything to every one" (1 Cor 15:28). The earthly liturgy we celebrate is our participation in that *actio Dei* or *actio Christi* in heaven.

## *Central Theme*

It is within this framework that we ought to understand the reasoning and the contents of the book *The Song of the Lamb: Sacred Music and the Heavenly Liturgy*, which is presented in the form of a conversation between its author, His Eminence Robert Cardinal Sarah, and Peter Carter, music director and sacred music enthusiast, for which I have been invited to write this foreword. I am grateful to His Eminence for the great love for liturgy that he carries within himself and for his profound sense of love for the Lord and His Church, which I had the good fortune to experience over many years in my association with him, as a co-worker and collaborator in both the then–Congregation for the Evangelization of Peoples and later in the Congregation for Divine Worship and the Discipline of the Sacraments, the curial department that oversees the liturgical life of the Church.

This book consists of fourteen chapters that deal with a series of pertinent questions on liturgy as a whole, its sublimity and importance for the life of the Church, and the threats and challenges it faces with the passage of time, and includes special considerations with regard to the subject of sacred music. Along with the subject of sacred music in general, this book considers the transformative value of Gregorian chant and congregational singing; the value of silence and contemplation, especially in relation to the correct understanding of actual participation in contrast to active participation; the value of the Latin language and the Second Vatican Council's insistence on Latin as the proper liturgical language of the Church, which has been largely ignored; issues of inculturation; the need to insist on a sense of the sacred; the importance of the role of priests and bishops for liturgical renewal; the importance of beauty vis-à-vis art and culture and its importance to evangelization; the importance of prioritizing sacred music and art as a means of divinizing humanity; the formation of vocations to the priesthood among those who love music; and the encouragement of the growth of expertise in sacred music and the role of choirs, especially the traditional boy choir. All of these discussions are put in the service of achieving a true spirit of renewal through intimacy with the Lord and His divine and eternal self, especially through devout and meaningful celebration of the liturgy. The case of the film *The Passion of the Christ* by Mel Gibson is presented as an example of how art can contribute to spiritual upliftment.

## *Basic Principles*

Cardinal Sarah has carefully presented the basic liturgical principles that should animate the development of sacred music, affirming clearly that liturgical action is "not merely an endeavor *by* the people of God; rather, it is the work of the Most Holy Trinity enacted *for* the people of God, the Church" (p. 27). In short, liturgical action is not to be created by us, but is "given" to us; we only participate in the heavenly assembly with Christ as the eternal Lamb. This is truly an affirmation of what was clearly stated in *Sacrosanctum concilium*, the Constitution on Sacred Liturgy of the Second Vatican Council. It affirms that "in the earthly liturgy, we take part in a foretaste of that heavenly liturgy which is celebrated in the holy city of Jerusalem toward which we journey as pilgrims, where Christ is sitting at the right hand of God, a minister of the holies and of the true tabernacle."[2] It clearly states, "No other person, even if he be a priest, may add, remove, or change anything in the liturgy on his own authority,"[3] indicating with how much seriousness we ought to consider our liturgical life.

The noble action of God in and through that of the celebrant is one of service and praise, which effects a salvific process of transformation in those who join in. Everything else contributes to this "tuning in", so to speak—to that eternal heavenly sacrifice of Christ, the Lamb that was slain and the Lamb that entered into communion with the Church as its bride (see Rev 21:9).

Cardinal Sarah then proceeds to outline what liturgical music is all about, and how and why it should not be confused with other types of music. True liturgical music transcends cultural and national boundaries, states the cardinal. Sacred music "should always orient us toward God" (p. 48). The book affirms further: "The essence of the liturgy is to confront and transform; it is about engaging with the very mystery of God. . . . There is a real danger in reducing the liturgy to a mere feel-good experience, as if the Church were offering a spiritual palliative on Sunday mornings" (p. 51). Insisting on Latin as the language of the liturgy, the cardinal states: "If we lose Latin then we lose a sense of the universality and shared liturgical culture that binds the Church together" (p. 59). We cancel, in a sense, our history and tradition, attempting to start everything anew. Stressing the vital role of Gregorian chant, upon which even the Second Vatican Council insisted, the cardinal affirms, "When listen-

[2] Vatican Council II, Constitution on the Sacred Liturgy *Sacrosanctum concilium* (December 4, 1963), no. 8.

[3] Ibid., no. 3.

ing to Gregorian chant, one can immediately sense that this music stems from an encounter with God. It is not merely a song, but a sung meditation, a musical contemplation of God" (p. 63).

### *Actual Participation*

This concept, introduced by Pope Pius X in his motu proprio *Tra le sollecitudini* of 1903, encouraged Gregorian chant as a means for the celebrative assembly to be more involved in what really takes place as a participation in the heavenly liturgy, especially in the celebration of the Eucharist and liturgical prayer. This was then reaffirmed by *Sacrosanctum concilium*, the Constitution on the Sacred Liturgy of the Second Vatican Council, which declares, "It is necessary that the faithful come to [the celebration of the sacred liturgy] with proper dispositions [recti animi dispositionibus], that their minds should be attuned to their voices, and that they should cooperate with divine grace lest they receive it in vain."[4]

Consequently, "Pastors of souls must . . . realize that, when the liturgy is celebrated, something more is required than the mere observation of the laws governing valid and licit celebration; it is their duty also to ensure that the faithful take part fully aware of what they are doing, actively engaged in the rite, and enriched by its effects."[5]

Liturgical scholar J. B. O'Connell welcomed the instruction of the Holy See on sacred music and the liturgy, which was dated September 3, 1958 and which opened the door to the active participation of the faithful in the liturgy. He stated: "The instruction by its wise and far-reaching provisions endeavours to bring the Liturgy from the cathedral,

[4] Ibid., no. 11.

[5] Ibid.

monastery and convent into the parish church. After more than a thousand years of passive attendance by the people at the Liturgy this will not be easy, and, obviously, the Church's desire for full active participation by the congregation in community worship can be attained only gradually, by carefully prepared stages, and with much patience and perseverance."[6]

This innovation was introduced to ensure that the laity did not remain mere spectators but were actively involved in the celebration. This rather limited invitation to the laity meant permitting a limited use of the vernacular, especially in the Scriptural readings, by encouraging the "dialogue Mass" and by calling for the people to sing those responses and parts of the Mass that pertain to them, including where possible, the daily proper chants.

This notion of active participation was meant to be an invitation for a limited participation of the laity and was reaffirmed by Vatican II when it stated: "The Church, therefore, earnestly desires that Christ's faithful, present at this mystery of faith, should not be there as strangers or silent spectators. On the contrary, through a proper appreciation of the rites and prayers they should participate knowingly, devoutly, and actively."[7] The word "actively" has often been understood in an exaggerated way to mean performing a lot of activities. Pope Benedict clarifies its meaning in *Sacramentum caritatis,* the post-synodal apostolic exhortation dated February 22, 2007: "It should be made clear that the word 'participation' does not refer to mere external activity during the celebration. In fact, the active participation called for by the

[6] J. B. O'Connell, introduction to *Sacred Music and Liturgy: The Instruction of the Sacred Congregation of Rites Concerning Sacred Music and Sacred Liturgy*, trans. and with a commentary by J. B. O'Connell (Newman Press, 1959), 14.

[7] *Sacrosanctum concilium*, no. 48, as translated in *The Documents of Vatican II*, ed. Walter M. Abbott, S.J. (The America Press, 1966), 154.

Council must be understood in more substantial terms, on the basis of a greater awareness of the mystery being celebrated and its relationship to daily life."[8] They should do so "not 'as strangers or silent spectators,' but as participants 'in the sacred action, conscious of what they are doing, actively and devoutly.'"[9] If this devoutness is abandoned to make the celebration a mere theater piece, it loses the full inner dynamism that it carries as the eschatological offering of Christ. Says Cardinal Sarah: "The rendering of *actuoso* as 'active' participation . . . has led many to assume that the faithful must be constantly *doing something*. This misconception reduces participation to mere physical activity and visible engagement. But this understanding is incomplete and fails to capture the essence of what Vatican II means by actual participation" (p. 76).

The cardinal moves on to discuss silence and its relationship to sacred music. Here the value of contemplation and its role in generating musical sensitivity is emphasized. Quoting Joseph Cardinal Ratzinger, the cardinal affirms: "When man comes into contact with God, mere speech is not enough. Areas of his existence are awakened that spontaneously turn into song. Indeed, man's own being is insufficient for what he has to express, and so he invites the whole of creation to become song with him."[10]

The study then moves on to the issue of liturgical language, which the Conciliar Constitution clearly affirmed to be Latin for the Latin rite.[11] While it wanted to make liturgy better understood and participated in, and thus permitted the limited use of the vernacular, "it also recognized Latin's

[8] *Sacramentum caritatis*, no. 52.

[9] Ibid., quoting *Sacrosanctum concilium*, no. 48.

[10] Joseph Cardinal Ratzinger, *The Spirit of the Liturgy* (Ignatius Press, 2000), 136.

[11] See *Sacrosanctum concilium*, no. 36.

irreplaceable value in both unifying the universal Church and preserving its ancient liturgical traditions" (p. 104). The letter issued by the Sacred Congregation for Divine Worship in 1974, *Voluntati obsequens,* was a plea by Pope Paul VI to preserve the use of at least some Latin in the liturgy.

## *Inculturation*

In this same light, the cardinal also discusses the most relevant issue of inculturation in the liturgy. While not denying the value of inculturation in the liturgy, the cardinal cautious the Church to approach it "with great care and discernment" (p. 117). As I see it, inculturation is indeed important and vital, as happened in the fourth century when a predominantly Greek-centered liturgy was turned into Latin. Inculturation is the way to a healthy enrichment of liturgy through sound adaptations. If correctly handled, it can lead us to an even deeper communion with Christ, for it recognizes the action of God in human history as a means for preparing the initial stages of evangelization of all these cultures. Sound principles, however, should guide these processes, as indicated in the instruction *Varietates legitimae* of the Congregation for Divine Worship and the Discipline of the Sacraments of January 25, 1994.

Naturally, one must be cautious to avoid any tendency toward syncretism. For example, the Eastern world religions that shape metaphysical thought patterns in our societies can offer the Church many new insights. These can help us touch the divine "otherness", in contrast to the Western nihilistic and materialistic philosophical orientations. This area needs, in my personal view, a deeper study.

The general background of all the answers given by His Eminence Robert Cardinal Sarah to the journalist interviewing him is the serious situation of the lack of a sense of the sacred, which is reflected in almost every aspect of sacred liturgy today. The world's movement away from God toward an increasingly immanent outlook on life is reflected in almost all the choices man makes. He is losing sight of the unending spiritual universe and the love of God manifest in the towering figure of Christ, in whose selfless sacrifice on the cross and victory over death are to be seen the transformation of humanity and its call to eternity. While the language of selfishness and sin is the problem afflicting society, liturgy seems to be reduced to mere showmanship, placing self at the center and not the Lord, without any consideration for what is happening in heaven, where the angels and saints continue to celebrate the redeeming sacrifice without end.

This materialistic, secularist orientation of life in the formerly Christian "North" is also discussed by His Eminence in chapter 8, and to some extent in chapter 9. These words of the cardinal are worthy of our reflection and study: "The widespread lack of faith and the eclipse of God and consequently the loss of the sense of the sacred in our secularized society has seeped into the Church herself. When the transcendent and divine nature of the liturgy is no longer understood or appreciated, it becomes easy to settle for mediocrity or even banality in our worship" (p. 172). The cardinal laments "resistance and even opposition to efforts to promote liturgical beauty and reverence" (p. 172). This is a sad situation indeed. For it is prayer that leads us to experience the Lord and generates faith in Him. And faith inspires us to true Christian witness, heroism, and holiness. The Church needs to become the haven or refuge for millions of men and women who are seeking the same values they have given up, albeit in an unknown way. This is especially true in a world—particularly in the Western hemisphere—taken over by materialism and secularism, with its greatest temptation being the rejection of God, or the so-called "death of God". This rejection also entails the rejection of the soul and the denial of the need for a heavenly salvation, and so it leads to an enslaving empty spirit of immanentism. The Church has to make a tangible expression of love, mercy, and of the call to return to God its greatest mission.

"Return to me with all your heart" (Joel 2:12) seems to be the voice they hear, but they do not know who calls them so lovingly. The Church needs to listen to those words of the Lord once again and commit herself more intensely to a process of re-evangelization of these societies with a strong accent on prayer, the dignified and conscious celebration of its liturgy, and a life of holiness: For, as the Lord says, "the harvest is plentiful, but the laborers are few" (Mt 10:37), and He wants us to pray to the Lord of the harvest rather than concentrating only on our efforts. Whether we can find true joy in the way we are proceeding is the all-important question.

January 6, 2025

# PREFACE

The writings of Cardinal Sarah, and especially his books with Nicolas Diat, have been a gift to the Church and have greatly contributed to my own spiritual nourishment. In 2019, I first interviewed Cardinal Sarah with Dr. Jennifer Donelson-Nowicka on the podcast *Square Notes: The Sacred Music Podcast*, and in 2021 I founded the Catholic Sacred Music Project with Dr. Timothy McDonnell, an organization that trains musicians to lead a revival of sacred music in their parishes and communities. Cardinal Sarah serves as the patron of this organization. In January of 2023 I approached him with the idea of collaborating on an interview book so that he could share his profound insights on prayer and the spiritual life in relation to the Church's tradition of sacred music. While this work is an effort to contribute to the liturgical and musical legacy of Pope Benedict XVI, we made an effort to avoid critiques and current debates over the use of particular liturgical books, leaving those discussions to other forums. Instead, the focus here is primarily to understand and communicate the Church's teaching on sacred music and its unbroken and living artistic tradition present in every legitimate form of the liturgy.

The contents of this book are a compilation of written responses to interview questions I submitted, as well as in-person interviews I had with His Eminence in June of 2023 and January of 2024. I am grateful to Charlie Deist, who helped me with transcribing the audio interviews, integrating the text of the written responses with those transcripts, and categorizing all of the content and presenting it in a logical format for this present publication. I have tried to present intact the words of Cardinal Sarah while editing the format in which they were initially given so as to provide a cohesive structure and flow in this present publication. Any shortcomings with the style or editing of this book remain my own.

Peter Carter
February 14, 2025

# Part I

# The Nature of the Liturgy

I

# LITURGY AND SACRED MUSIC

PETER CARTER: *Your Eminence, when did your appreciation and passion for sacred music first emerge?*

ROBERT CARDINAL SARAH: My journey with sacred music began during my formative years at the minor seminary of Saint Augustine, in the Ivory Coast, where I commenced my studies at the age of twelve. Music played an integral role in our seminary education, thanks to the presence of Father Pierre Messner, a holy priest and skilled musician. He introduced me to music theory, solfège (a method for learning how to read music where each note is associated with a particular syllable), and the beauty of Gregorian chant and polyphonic singing, which have the ability to elevate the soul toward God and open the heart to His mystery.

Later, my time at the Major Seminary in Nancy, France, proved to be a deeply formative experience, allowing me to immerse myself in the profound mystery of my priestly vocation and to connect with God through the daily liturgies and sacred music. One moment in the liturgy that has always filled me with joy is the singing of the Creed, knowing that we proclaim the same beliefs and sing the same melodies that Christians have sung for centuries. This participation in professing the same faith as the early Christians is truly remarkable! When we sing or recite the Creed, we can hear their voices and with conviction profess the same faith for which many of them sacrificed their own lives.

Professing the Creed creates a powerful connection between all Christians, past and present, and affirms that our Christian faith is not merely a legend but a historical reality: God truly became man out of love for us, died, and rose from the dead—a truth to which we bear witness (cf. Acts 5:30–32). Year after year, the singing of the Creed and other sacred chants has gradually drawn me deeper into the liturgical prayer that is the Eucharistic Sacrifice. They have aided me in experiencing and participating in the immense and resplendent majesty and holiness of God while guiding and enriching my priestly vocation. And through my participation in the sacred liturgy, I cooperate with Christ and His will for the salvation of the world.

*Can you elaborate on the role and significance of music within the context of Christian worship?*

Music has been an integral part of worship and culture from the earliest days of Christian worship, and even before that, during the time of the Temple in Jerusalem. The Gospels testify that even our Lord sang hymns in prayer. And Saint Paul exhorts the faithful of Ephesus to "be filled with the Spirit, addressing one another in psalms and hymns and spiritual songs, singing and making melody to the Lord with all your heart, always and for everything giving thanks in the name of our Lord Jesus Christ to God the Father" (Eph 5:18–20).

However, when we seek to define music, it can seem elusive. We know intuitively that music conveys what words cannot express. One commonly held idea of art in general, and music in particular, is that it serves an ornamental function. Art, in this view, is an *addition* to beautify what is made; it does not, in fact, touch the essence of the thing to be embellished. Thus, a building is first constructed and then adorned, with the walls whitewashed to hang paintings or artworks. But this conception reveals a superficial understanding of artistic work and its creation from various points of view. Michelangelo, standing before a block of marble, already envisioned his marvelous sculpture, which simply had to be revealed through his skilled striking of the hammer and chisel. The work and its beauty were already present; he, the artist, unveiled it. Contemporary theology, particularly the theological-philosophical speculation of Joseph Ratzinger, has opened our eyes to a broader and more fascinating reality. Sacred music—when it is true art—is an epiphany: It signifies a divine manifestation through its revelation of Beauty. In sculpture, music, and poetry, He who is Beauty is incarnate in the artistic form, though in a much less full and substantive manner than in the Eucharist or in the manger at Bethlehem. As Cardinal Ratzinger wrote in 1986:

> The Word becoming music is on the one hand sensualization, incarnation, the attraction of pre-rational and trans-rational forces, the attraction of the hidden sound of creation, and the uncovering of the song that lies at the base of things. But this musification is also itself now the site of the shift in the movement: it is not only the incarnation of the Word, but at the same time the spiritualization of the flesh.[1]

This perspective underscores humanity's non-angelic nature—that of flesh and blood—highlighting the need for a tangible domain where human spirituality can develop and express itself, while recognizing that humans possess an embodied soul:

> Liturgical music is a result of the claim and the dynamics of the Word's incarnation. For incarnation means that also among us the Word cannot be just speech. To begin

[1] Pope Benedict XVI, *A New Song for the Lord* (Crossroad Publishing Company, 2013), 154.

> with, the sacramental signs themselves are certainly the central way in which the incarnation continues to work. But they would be homeless if they were not immersed in a liturgy that as a whole follows this extension of the Word into the physical and into the sphere of all our senses. The right to have images—indeed their necessity—comes from this in contrast to the Jewish and Islamic types of worship. And from this also comes the necessity to call on those deeper realms of understanding and response that reveal themselves in music. Faith becoming music is a part of the process of the Word becoming flesh.[2]

The Church teaches that God is truly present in various liturgical actions: in the Divine Office, in the proclamation of the Word that begins the Eucharistic celebration, and most preeminently in the Eucharistic elements of consecrated bread and wine. But this same God, who has promised to abide with us until the end of the age, also subtly reveals His immense beauty and aspects of His very essence through genuine works of art and music.

Music exists in myriad forms, with a vast spectrum of origins and quality. There is music for entertainment, leisure, and dancing, ranging from popular to classical genres and even extending to what one might call diabolical music. Each of these expressions reflects a distinct reality. Sacred music, however, finds its wellspring in the Holy Spirit, in the revelation of God's Word, and in the unveiling of the eternal Logos. Only this music is fitting for the Church's liturgy and life. Sacred music contains various musical expressions, born from the same spiritual source but manifested in diverse contexts and historical periods, while all meeting the Church's criteria for music it considers sacred. Furthermore, beyond what is strictly understood as sacred or liturgical music, there exist other musical forms that still uphold

[2] Ibid., 153–54.

aspects of the standards of sacred music while not always being appropriate in form or style for liturgical worship. Music in this category may share the same divine origin and thus be suitable for a person's spiritual life in devotional prayer even if the music is not always liturgically appropriate. Each musical composition is evaluated and deemed *liturgically* appropriate on the basis of the criteria that the Church has set forth in her documents on sacred music.

## *The Liturgy as the Work of the Trinity*

*You mention the appropriateness of certain types of music for the sacred liturgy. This is a central concern of our discussion, and certainly an area of current debate within the Church. How should we understand the liturgy and its role in the life of the Church?*

When we discuss liturgy, we often limit our understanding to the specific moments of worship within the Church's life—the rites and ceremonies that comprise our prayers, sacraments, and communal observances. However, the term "liturgy", derived from the Ancient Greek *leitourgia*, invites us to embrace a more expansive view. This term historically referred to the acts of service performed freely by Greek nobles on behalf of the community. It signified a public work done for the benefit of the people. In its fullest Christian sense, therefore, the grand liturgy is not merely an endeavor *by* the People of God; rather, it is the work of the Most Holy Trinity enacted *for* the People of God, the Church. The liturgy emerges not as human creation or activity, but as "opus Trinitatis"—the work of the Trinity—permeating the life of the Church at large. We must be careful not to reduce the liturgy to a mere human endeavor, as if we were the creators of the liturgy. As suggested by its etymology, it serves the people not as something crafted by them, but rather as a divine offering of the Son to the Father on behalf of Christ's spouse, the Church, making possible our participation in the divine reality.

As I reflected in 2015 in my book *God or Nothing*, "During my years as a seminarian, and then after my ordination, my certainty was strengthened. I understood that the greatest way to be with the Son of God made man was still the liturgy. At Mass the priest is face to face with God. The Mass is the most important thing in our lives. And the Divine Office, the breviary, prepares us for it."[3]

*So the Mass is the most important thing in our lives?*

Yes! Allow me to share with you the beautiful words of Pope Benedict XVI, who eloquently expressed the absolute priority of the liturgy in the preface to the Russian language edition of his book "The Spirit of the Liturgy":

> *Nihil Opera Dei praeponatur*, let nothing be preferred before the Work of God. With these words, Saint Benedict, in his *Rule* (43.3), established the absolute priority of Divine Worship over every other duty of the monastic life. This maxim, even in the monastic life, did not turn out to be immediately obvious, because for the monks their work in agriculture and in learning was also an essential duty. Both in agriculture and also in handicrafts and in the work of formation there could certainly be pressing temporal matters that might appear to be more important than the liturgy. Faced with all this, Benedict, in assigning priority to the liturgy, unequivocally highlights the priority of God himself in our life: "At the hour of Divine Office, as soon as the signal has been heard, let the monk leave whatever he may have in hand and make great haste, but with due gravity" (43.1).

[3] Robert Cardinal Sarah, *God or Nothing* (Ignatius Press, 2015), 51.

> In the consciousness of people nowadays, the things of God and, consequently, the liturgy do not appear urgent at all. . . . If God is no longer important, the criteria for deciding what is important shift. In setting God aside, man subjects himself to constraints that make him the slave of material forces and that thus are opposed to his dignity.
>
> In the year following the Second Vatican Council, I became conscious once again of the priority of God and of the Divine Liturgy. The misunderstanding of the liturgical reform that spread widely in the Catholic Church led to an increasing prominence of the aspect of instruction and of one's own activity and creativity. The doings of men almost made us forget the presence of God. In such a situation, it became increasingly clear that the existence of the Church is vitally dependent on the correct celebration of the liturgy and that the Church is in danger when the primacy of God no longer appears in the liturgy and thus in life. . . . The true renewal of the liturgy is a fundamental prerequisite for the renewal of the Church.[4]

These words serve as a profound reminder that the sacred liturgy is not merely a human activity, but a divine encounter that transcends our earthly understanding. It is the very source and summit of our Christian life, drawing us into the mystical presence of God Himself.

*Can you expand on this idea of the liturgy as a transcendent, mystical encounter and a participation in the life of the Trinity?*

When I approach the Mass, I truly encounter the sacred. I stand directly before the Divine Presence in the Word, the proclamation of Scripture, and through the visible and tangible signs of the consecrated bread and wine. What exists

[4] Benedict XVI, *What Is Christianity? The Last Writings*, trans. Michael J. Miller, ed. Elio Guerriero and Georg Gänswein (Ignatius Press, 2023), 57–58.

before me is the most sacred of things, the very standard of holiness: God Himself. The logic of the Old Testament held that the holy (*kadosh* in Hebrew) belonged solely to the realm of God, while human existence remained entirely profane. However, everything associated with the Temple—the sacrificial animals, temple vessels, even people—could be set apart and consecrated to the Divine. Yet Christ's Incarnation sanctifies our very nature—the Holy God dwelt among us, sanctifying even ordinary human activities. Nevertheless, the Mass retains a distinctly sacred character apart from the mundane world that has been elevated in dignity through the Incarnation.

The Gospel accounts of the Last Supper clearly convey its sacredness. Christ prepared a dignified place for the first Mass, chose the festive day of Passover, and invited the presence of a few chosen disciples. At the Last Supper, everything was carefully considered and set apart, distinct from the profane and the mundane. When Christ uttered those eternal words over the bread and wine, transforming them into His Body and Blood, He instituted the unfathomable gift that perpetually connects earth to heaven. The words of Saint Paul concerning the Last Supper are filled with solemnity: "For I received from the Lord what I also delivered to you, that the Lord Jesus on the night when he was betrayed took bread, and when he had given thanks, he broke it, and said, 'This is my body, which is for you. Do this in remembrance of me.' In the same way also the chalice, after supper, saying, 'This chalice is the new covenant in my blood. Do this, as often as you drink it, in remembrance of me'" (1 Cor 11:23–25).

The memorial of the Lord's Supper that we celebrate makes present the central moment of the history of salvation, brought by Jesus Christ with His death, Resurrection, and Ascension. By celebrating the Eucharist, we truly relive, not in a figurative or symbolic sense, that Paschal Sacrifice. We participate and are inwardly transformed. The memorial of the ancient covenants—that of Noah, Abraham, and Moses—gives way to the New and Eternal Covenant, accomplished by Christ on the cross, just as the prophet Jeremiah had announced:

> Behold, the days are coming, says the LORD, when I will make a new covenant with the house of Israel and the house of Judah, not like the covenant which I made with their fathers when I took them by the hand to bring them out of the land of Egypt, my covenant which they broke, and I showed myself their Master, says the LORD. But this is the covenant which I will make with the house of Israel after those days, says the LORD: I will put my law within them, and I will write it upon their hearts; and I will be their God, and they shall be my people. (Jer 31:31–33)

Through the celebration of Easter, the eternal Trinity invites mankind to participate in its inner life, thereby forming the Church. As Saint Cyprian proudly affirms, "De unitate Patris et Filii et Spiritus Sancti plebs adunata" ("The people gathered in the unity of the Father, Son, and Holy Spirit").[5] This great liturgy is accomplished by the Most Holy Trinity itself.

## *"Without Sunday, We Cannot Live"*

*Today, we sometimes witness a casual attitude toward the Mass that seems to forget its sacred character. How does this contrast with the experience of the Mass by the early Church?*

It is crucial to remember the reverence, astonishment, and love with which these early believers approached the Sunday

[5] Saint Cyprian, *De Oratione Domenica, Part 1: The Text* (George Bell & Sons, 1907), no. 23, p. 19.

Eucharist, viewing it as the "weekly Easter". For them, the Eucharist was not merely a part of their Christian identity but the very heart of their community's life and mission. So central and vital was the Eucharist to these early Christians that they were willing to risk death rather than forgo its celebration. An example of this dedication can be found in the year 304, during the reign of Emperor Diocletian, who issued an edict prohibiting Christians from possessing Scriptures, gathering on Sundays for the Eucharist, or constructing places of worship, all under pain of death. In the small town of Abitene, in present-day Tunisia, forty-nine Christians were discovered assembling in the house of Octavius Felix, defying the imperial decree by celebrating the Eucharist on a Sunday. They were arrested and brought to Carthage for interrogation by Proconsul Anulinus. When questioned by the proconsul as to why they had violated the emperor's strict command, one of them replied, "Sine dominico non possumus", meaning "Without Sunday, we cannot live." These faithful believers understood that without the Sunday Eucharist, they would lack the strength to face the daily challenges and trials of life. After enduring horrific tortures, these forty-nine martyrs of Abitene were put to death, confirming their faith through the shedding of their blood. Today, we remember and reverence them in the glory of the risen Christ, their sacrifice a testament to the depth of their love for the Eucharist.

For these early Christians, no other aspect of their faith life—whether it be community gatherings, acts of charity, or tending to the sick—could replace their participation in the Eucharistic celebration, for which they willingly gave their lives. After the example of Christ Himself, they sought to sanctify their daily actions out of love for God. Yet, it was only in the Holy Mass that they could truly receive the Incarnate Word, the source and summit of their Christian life. This was seen as an embodiment of the Christian community's identity and the heart of its life and mission.

*Your Eminence, in describing the meaning of the "liturgy", you noted we often limit our understanding of it solely to the rites and ceremonies of religious worship, such as Sunday Mass. Yet, you suggest its scope encompasses Christ's divine worship of the Father, through which we can understand the fullness of the Church's essence and mission. Could you elaborate on what other dimensions of the Church's life fall under this broader liturgical paradigm?*

The most comprehensive definition of liturgy can be found in *Sacrosanctum concilium*, the Second Vatican Council's Constitution on the Sacred Liturgy. It states that "in Christ 'the perfect achievement of our reconciliation came forth, and the fullness of divine worship was given to us.'"[6] This wording underscores the centrality of Christ in the liturgy, and is borrowed from the *Sacramentarium Veronense*, one of the oldest surviving sacramentaries of the Roman Rite dating back to the sixth or seventh century.

The wondrous works of God among the people of the Old Testament were but a prelude to the work of Christ the Lord in redeeming mankind and giving perfect glory to God. He achieved His task principally by the Paschal Mystery of His blessed Passion, Resurrection from the dead, and glorious Ascension, whereby "dying he has destroyed our death, and by rising, restored our life"[7]. For it was from

[6] Vatican Council II, Constitution on the Sacred Liturgy *Sacrosanctum concilium* (December 4, 1963), no. 5, quoting *Sacramentarium Veronense* (ed. Mohlberg), no. 1265.

[7] *The Roman Missal* (Latin text, Libreria Editrice Vaticana, 2008; English

the side of Christ as He slept the sleep of death upon the cross that there came forth "the wondrous sacrament of the whole Church"[8].

As the Scriptures proclaim, Christ is the sole mediator between God and men. Thus, the liturgy is the shared action of Christ and His Body, the Church, exercising the priesthood of Jesus Christ through visible and sensory signs. "Christ indeed always associates the Church with Himself in this great work wherein God is perfectly glorified and men are sanctified. The Church is His beloved Bride who calls to her Lord, and through Him offers worship to the Eternal Father."[9] To carry out this great work, Christ is always present in the life of the Church, and especially in her celebrations of the sacred liturgy. He is present in the Sacrifice of the Mass, not only in the person of His minister but particularly under the Eucharistic species. "From this it follows that every liturgical celebration, because it is an action of Christ the priest and His Body which is the Church, is a sacred action surpassing all others; no other action of the Church can equal its efficacy by the same title and to the same degree."[10] These ideas, though professed by all Catholic believers, are truly astonishing. Yet, they are merely the beginning of the miraculous nature of the liturgy, which encompasses the vision of eternal life in heaven.

---

translation, International Commission on English in the Liturgy Corporation, 2010), 558

[8] *Sacrosanctum concilium*, no. 5, quoting prayer before the second lesson for Holy Saturday, as it was in the Roman Missal before the restoration of Holy Week.

[9] Ibid., no. 7.

[10] Ibid., no. 7.

*As I contemplate what you have said about the liturgy as the work of Christ on behalf of His Bride, the Church, I am struck by a seeming paradox: We participate here and now in the unending heavenly liturgy, yet we are also waiting for the ultimate face-to-face encounter in heaven. How do you reconcile the profound but incomplete communion we experience through earthly rites with the heavenly worship of God?*

The earthly liturgy serves as a pledge of the eternal heavenly liturgy within the holy city, the New Jerusalem. It embodies a mystical heaven on earth, offering us a genuine participation in the ceaseless heavenly liturgy. The Constitution on the Sacred Liturgy elaborates on this connection, stating that "In the earthly liturgy we take part in a foretaste of that heavenly liturgy which is celebrated in the holy city of Jerusalem . . . where Christ is sitting at the right hand of God, a minister of the holies and of the true tabernacle; we sing a hymn to the Lord's glory with all the warriors of the heavenly army; venerating the memory of the saints, we hope for some part and fellowship with them; we eagerly await the Saviour, Our Lord Jesus Christ, until He, our life, shall appear and we too will appear with Him in glory."[11] This earthly liturgy, therefore, stands as the gate of heaven, through which the Triune God reaches out to us, and we, in turn, go out to meet Him. The Church draws her life from the liturgy, which is "the summit toward which the activity of the Church is directed" and "the font from which all her power flows".[12]

Joseph Ratzinger, reflecting on the eschatological vision of the liturgy, highlights the paradox of a seemingly defeated

[11] Ibid., no. 8.

[12] Ibid., no. 10.

earthly Church ultimately triumphing through the Lamb's victory: "The paradox now becomes even more powerful. It is not the gigantic beasts of prey, with their power over the media and their technical strength, who win the victory. No, it is the sacrificed Lamb that conquers. And so once again, definitely, there resounds the song of God's servant Moses, which has now become the song of the Lamb."[13]

He references the vision of the Church in Revelation "standing beside the sea of glass with harps of God in their hands. And they sing the song of Moses, the servant of God, and the song of the Lamb" (Rev 15:2–3). But what is this "song of the Lamb", this "new song" (Rev 14:3)? As singing befits the lover, as Saint Augustine reminds us, this new song is that of the Church, washed and regenerated by baptism, for Christ, her spouse. In the Gospel of John, during the Feast of Tabernacles, Jesus stood up and cried out, "If anyone thirst, let him come to me and drink. He who believes in me, as the Scripture has said, 'Out of his heart shall flow rivers of living water'" (Jn 7:37–38). It is He who will provide this water, for "a river of the water of life, bright as crystal, [flows] from the throne of God and of the Lamb" (Rev 22:1). In the New Jerusalem, our earthly forms of worship will fade: There will be no temple, lamp, or sunlight" (see Rev 21:22–23). "They shall see God", Saint Matthew writes (Mt 5:8). In the meantime, we should strive to sing the hymn of the Lamb not merely with our tongues, but with our lives—or, as expressed in a beautiful inscription in the village church of Saint Magnus in Anloo, in the Netherlands, "non cordula sed cor psallit

[13] Joseph Cardinal Ratzinger, *The Spirit of the Liturgy* (Ignatius Press, 2000), 137.

in aure Dei": We sing not with stringed instruments, but with hearts that resonate in the ear of God.

In our earthly pilgrimage to this promised land, our participation in this worship is through signs and symbols—as if "in a mirror dimly" . We look forward with faith and hope to that joyful "face to face" encounter, as Saint Paul says (1 Cor 13:12), when we shall behold God "as he is" (cf. 1 Jn 3:2).

2

# THE CRITERIA FOR SACRED MUSIC

## Tra le sollecitudini: *The Magna Carta of Sacred Music*

PETER CARTER: *What are the principles or criteria that the Church gives for music to be considered appropriate for liturgical celebrations?*

ROBERT CARDINAL SARAH: The criteria for determining the suitability of music for liturgical use were established by Pope Saint Pius X in his motu proprio *Tra le sollecitudini* (On Sacred Music), which has been regarded as a Magna Carta for sacred music since its promulgation in 1903. This document has been foundational in every document on sacred music that the Church has written since then. The key passage of *Tra le sollecitudini* outlines three essential criteria for sacred music: "Sacred music should consequently possess, in the highest degree, the qualities proper to the liturgy, and in particular sanctity and goodness of form, which will spontaneously produce the final quality of universality."[1] By insisting on sanctity as the first criterion, Saint Pius X excludes all music that is profane in style, form, or expression from the liturgy and insists that all sacred music must possess the highest degree of beauty and artistic integrity, which will then naturally embody a "universal" or "catholic" character.

[1] Pope Pius X, motu proprio *Tra le sollecitudini* (On Sacred Music) (November 22, 1903), no. 2, https://adoremus.org/1903/11/tra-le-sollecitudini/.

*For those who may be unfamiliar with the term, a motu proprio is a document issued by the Pope on his own initiative and personally signed by him, signifying the great importance of the matter to the pope for the whole Church. What was the historical context that led to the creation of this document, and how did these three criteria come about?*

In the wake of the French Revolution, the Church faced numerous challenges in rebuilding her institutions and reasserting her cultural influence. The political and social upheavals of the late eighteenth and nineteenth centuries were predominantly anticlerical and possessed a focus on the secularization of society, creating a social atmosphere that was not conducive to the flourishing of sacred art and music. By the time of Saint Pius X's ascension to the papacy, the state of sacred music had become heavily influenced by the secular and profane music of the opera and theater, rather than the sacred culture of the Church influencing the secular culture. *Tra le sollecitudini* condemned the use of operatic and theatrical music in the church, saying that such music was not sacred in itself and thus was not appropriate to be used in the liturgy.

When he was a cardinal, Giuseppe Sarto had already initiated efforts to reform sacred music during his tenure as patriarch of Venice in collaboration with Father Angelo De Santi and Italian composer Lorenzo Perosi. When he was elected pope, taking the name Pius X, the document he had prepared for the Archdiocese of Venice was released to the entire Church, helping to inspire a widespread renewal of sacred music. As a result, operatic music, band music, drums, nightingale organ stops, and other theatrical effects were explicitly prohibited in liturgical settings.

## *Criterion No. 1: Sanctity*

*We might draw a parallel between the operatic music of the nineteenth and early twentieth centuries and certain modern "themed Masses" that incorporate popular musical styles such as folk, pop, jazz, and rock. On what basis does* Tra le sollecitudini *exclude this kind of music from the liturgy?*

Elaborating on the first criterion of sanctity, Pope Saint Pius X states, "It must be holy, and must, therefore, exclude all profanity not only in itself, but in the manner in which it is presented by those who execute it."[2] Here, the term "profanity" takes on a different meaning from our common understanding of obscenity, rather referring to anything that is secular and not distinctly sacred. This distinction does not pass artistic judgment on music that fails to meet the requirement of sanctity, but rather indicates that such music is more suitable for use "outside the temple".

In his apostolic exhortation *Sacramentum caritatis*, Pope Benedict XVI asserts that "as far as the liturgy is concerned, we cannot say that one song is as good as another."[3] While we may intuitively understand this on some level, how do we concretely discern what is appropriate for the liturgy? How do we draw the line between what is sacred and what is profane, and how can we avoid prioritizing our own subjective preferences when making this discernment? To begin with, we must acknowledge the genuine distinction between the sacred and the profane. Failing to recognize this distinction will inevitably lead to the profanation of the sacred. Moreover, we must be aware of our own preferences

[2] Ibid., no. 2.

[3] Benedict XVI, apostolic exhortation *Sacramentum caritatis* (The Sacrament of Charity) (February 22, 2007), no. 42.

and desires and be willing to set them aside if they are not worthy of the temple. Just as Moses removed his sandals when approaching the burning bush where God resided on Mount Sinai, we too must approach liturgical prayer with humility and reverence. Liturgical worship is never about asserting our own preferences or style of worshiping God. Rather than reflecting ourselves or the things of the world, that which is sacred must reflect the sacredness of God Himself. The best approach in this discernment is to open our hearts and humbly listen to God, allowing Him to teach us how to pray, just as He taught Moses in the Old Testament and His disciples in the New Testament.

## *Criterion No. 2: Goodness of Form*

*The next criterion that Saint Pius X gives us is "goodness of form". What is meant by this and what is its importance for sacred music?*

The concept of "goodness of form" underscores the need for the liturgy to be marked by beauty, and for liturgical music to draw people toward God, rather than toward the musicians or the virtuosic performance of the musicians. As Pope Benedict XVI says in *Sacramentum caritatis*, "Everything related to the Eucharist should be marked by beauty."[4] Pope Saint Pius X elaborates on this point in paragraph 2 of *Tra le sollecitudini*: "It must be true art, for otherwise it will be impossible for it to exercise on the minds of those who listen to it that efficacy which the Church aims at obtaining in admitting into her liturgy the art of musical sounds."

Given the classical Thomistic understanding of beauty prevalent at the time, Pope Saint Pius X did not feel the need to elaborate at great length on this concept. According

[4] Ibid., no. 41.

to Saint Thomas Aquinas, beauty consists of three essential elements: proportion (the harmonious relationship among parts), integrity (the coherence of the whole), and splendor or brightness (the radiant and attractive power of truth).[5]

*In today's world, there is much debate surrounding the concept of "truth", with many denying the existence of absolute truth. It is often said that beauty is purely subjective, or that "beauty is in the eye of the beholder." In the context of sacred music, how can we discern what is true, good, and beautiful? Is beauty simply in the ear of the listener, or is beauty indeed objective?*

In contemporary society, everyone claims their own subjective truth, leading some to be content with the idea that their personal conceptions of beauty and truth are not universally shared. However, as Christians, we must ask ourselves: Who can teach us what is true? Only the one who said, "I am the Truth" (see Jn 14:6). If we encounter many competing "truths" within the Church, it is because Christians have not fully embraced the one Truth that is Christ. He teaches us everything that is true, good, and beautiful. As Catholics, we must listen attentively to Christ, who reveals the truth not only to individuals but to all.

Whereas discerning truth in moral theology is usually more straightforward, building on logical principles, discerning objective beauty in music can appear to be more complex because of the experiential nature of music existing in time. While one might say something is beautiful on the basis of subjective personal perception, it is also possible to discern objective beauty in sacred music through analyzing its musical and harmonic structure.

Liturgically, the best criterion is this: Does it conform to

[5] See, for example, *Summa Theologiae* I, q. 5 art. 4, ad 1.

and serve the nature and end of the liturgy, the worship of God, and the consequent sanctification of man? The primary function of sacred music is not to represent worldly culture or personal expression, but to give glory to God and to elevate the person to God. The measure of good sacred music, therefore, lies in how effectively it fulfills this function. The doctrines of the Church can assist us in distinguishing between what is true and good, and what is not. However, the discernment of beauty calls for a contemplation of God's attributes. This contemplation is a form of artistic formation, especially relevant in the liturgy, where music of the highest artistic expression must be employed. Truly beautiful art should represent the pinnacle of artistic expression, having a timelessness that transcends personal experience and cultural barriers. If art were purely subjective, it would be impossible for a musical piece to be universally cherished and enjoyed. Rather, it is because true art has a divine origin, reflecting the beauty and truth that flow from God Himself, that it has a universal and timeless appeal.

Cardinal Ratzinger, in his writings from the year 2000, eloquently expresses this concept:

> In virtue of his work in creation, the Logos is, therefore, called the "art of God" (*ars = technē*!). The Logos himself is the great artist, in whom all works of art—the beauty of the universe—have their origin. To sing with the universe means, then, to follow the track of the Logos and to come close to him. All true human art is an assimilation to *the* artist, to Christ, to the mind of the Creator.[6]

This insight reveals that all authentic art finds its source in the divine *Logos*, the creative Word of God. When we

[6] Joseph Cardinal Ratzinger, *The Spirit of the Liturgy* (Ignatius Press, 2000), 153–54.

engage with true art, whether through creation or appreciation, we are participating in a sacred act, drawing closer to Christ and the beauty of His creation.

However, it is true that the ability to appreciate and discern the quality of a work of art is, to a certain extent, a matter of education and cultural formation. Just as an illiterate person might view a written poem as mere marks on a page, those who have not been formed in the understanding of sacred music may struggle to recognize its inherent beauty. And while the Church provides guidance in distinguishing between what is true, good, and beautiful and what is not, she does not give us a definitive formula for determining the nature of beauty in music in the way that a computer algorithm might. Rather, the Church gives us principles that require a contemplative approach, a prayerful consideration of God's attributes and how they are reflected in the music.

## *Criterion No. 3: Universality*

*This brings us to the third and final criterion of universality. How does* Tra le sollecitudini *define this concept?*

Pope Saint Pius X emphasizes that liturgical music, in addition to being sacred and true art, must be universal: "While every nation is permitted to admit into its ecclesiastical compositions those special forms which may be said to constitute its native music, still these forms must be subordinated in such a manner to the general characteristics of sacred music that nobody of any nation may receive an impression other than good on hearing them."[7] To enter truly into the Church's liturgical tradition, we must recognize that the liturgy itself is something passed down and given to us, not something to be created anew with each generation or

[7] *Tra le sollecitudini*, no. 2.

culture. The liturgical books are not mere collections of historical texts; they are the embodiment of the Church's liturgical tradition surrounding the sacraments instituted by Christ Himself. The liturgical books represent an organic development of the liturgy that is rooted in tradition yet open to legitimate developments of local culture, while always in accordance with the liturgical rubrics. By immersing ourselves in the Church's liturgical tradition, we free ourselves from the burden of having to "create" the sacred. Instead, we are invited to partake in the beauty and wisdom that has been shaped and refined over the centuries, allowing us to worship God not in isolation, but in communion with the entire Church over the centuries—past, present, and future.

The Church's liturgical tradition is not a relic of the past. It is a living stream that nourishes and sustains our faith. To enter into this tradition is to immerse oneself in a centuries-old conversation between God and His people. It is not a task of expressing something of ourselves that is new, but rather one of discovery and participation. While the repertoire and performance of sacred music has evolved over time and will continue to do so, its core principles and teachings have remained steadfast throughout the centuries. These teachings, akin to the Church's doctrines, may be clarified and expanded upon, but their essence remains unchanging, like God Himself. The beauty and truth expressed in liturgical music from any era can remain universally accessible, retaining its value and relevance today, regardless of whether it was composed centuries ago or in the present decade.

True liturgical music transcends cultural and national boundaries, offering a universal language that speaks of the sacred. This universality does not negate the beauty of local expressions but rather enriches them and is enriched by them. By embracing the universality of sacred music, we unite our voices with those of the faithful around the world and throughout history, joining in the eternal hymn of praise that the Church continually offers to God.

## *The Allure of Popular Music*

*Pope Saint Pius X gives the criterion of universality in the same paragraph in which he introduces sanctity and goodness of form, noting that even while musical styles differ across cultures, liturgical music should not offend the sense of the sacred. However, in the past sixty years or so, we have witnessed numerous examples of musical styles originating outside of the Church being incorporated into the liturgy, such as folk music, pop music, musical theater, and, to lesser degrees, rock and roll, jazz, polka, etc., and some of this music is still present in parishes and cathedrals today. The genre of praise and worship music is a particularly popular style of religious music that closely resembles American pop music. Personally, I've observed that people often lean toward musical styles with a broad and commercial appeal, even if they possess less authentic beauty and less musical integrity. For instance, in my home state of New Jersey, where music is widely appreciated, the music sung and performed in churches often mirrors Broadway or Disney tunes, albeit with religious lyrics. What would you say to those who enjoy these styles of music and want to use them to praise God? Do these styles of music have a place in the liturgy even if they do not correspond to a strict understanding of the three principles of sacred music: sanctity, goodness of form (or beauty), and universality?*

First, it is important to recognize that not everything that makes us feel good is suitable for worship. Sitting on cushions may feel more comfortable than kneeling on wood! If the style of sacred music closely resembles what we hear in secular culture, it may make us feel good because it is familiar, but it does not necessarily dispose us toward prayer. Sacred music should always orient us toward God and foster a participation in the liturgy that is primarily internal and spiritual. Only then can we express our adoration in a manner that is both external and physical, truly joining with the choirs of angels singing around the throne of heaven.

Secondly, everything that approaches the liturgy must be truly sacred in all its elements, just as Moses had to remove his sandals when he approached the burning bush. The same principle applies to liturgical music. As Pope Benedict XVI (then Cardinal Ratzinger) stated in his book *The Spirit of the Liturgy*: "Not every kind of music can have a place in Christian worship."[8] A significant portion of current pop music is often physical and sensual, primarily engaging the body. The music is often dominated by a strong and regular beat, while Gregorian chant and the polyphony of the Renaissance usually possess a rhythm that is subservient to the rhythm of the text that the music is trying to express. The rhythmic dominance in pop music may be advantageous for activities that are inherently physical, such as dancing, allowing someone listening to the song for the first time to easily move to it. While this may be a good thing for dancing, liturgical music should engage us not primarily physically, but spiritually, leading us to pray (movement of the soul) rather than to dance (movement of the body).

*I think in most cases, the incorporation of popular music styles into the liturgy is often accommodated by the clergy out of a well-intentioned (if misguided) attempt to be pastoral and to give musicians an opportunity to sing and play the music they know in service to the Church, even if the style is not uniquely sacred. Can we make a distinction*

[8] Ratzinger, *Spirit of the Liturgy*, 151.

*between "popular" music in general and "pop music" or other commercial genres that are more obviously secular in style?*

Pope Benedict XVI offered a profound perspective on this matter in one of his reflections, "Sing Artistically for God",[9] an essay that highlights the incompatibility of rock and pop music with the Church's liturgy. His argument centered on the fundamental differences between pop music, which targets mass society, and folk music, which is the traditional expression of a cohesive community shaped by shared language, history, and lifestyle. He notes that pop music aligns with the culture of the masses, focusing on quantity, production, and success. It is part of a culture that values what is measurable and marketable, catering to the lowest common denominator to avoid upsetting anyone—or, on the other hand, deeply engaging anyone. This culture demands instant gratification without cost, work, or effort, which is fundamentally incompatible with the culture of the Gospel. The Gospel seeks to free us from the tyranny of money, constant activity, and mediocrity, leading us toward the discipline of truth—something pop music avoids. Similarly, rock music leads to "sensory intoxication" and a sense of "losing oneself", which is the opposite of the goal of Christian worship, which aims for inward conversion and recognition of God's presence.

On the other hand, folk music of a high quality may become sacralized, like the Greco-Roman pillars present in much sacred architecture, and find an appropriate place in liturgical use. However, rock music and certain pop genres must be excluded due to their inherent nature. The subtitle

[9] In Pope Benedict XVI (Joseph Ratzinger), *A New Song for the Lord* (Crossroad Publishing Company, 2013), 119–37.

Ratzinger wrote for this part of his essay is indicative of the reason: "Against Pastoral Pragmatism as an End in Itself". He pointedly asked, "Is it a pastoral success when we are capable of following the trend of mass culture and thus share the blame for its making people immature or irresponsible?"[10] The choice of liturgical music is not merely a matter of personal preference or pastoral pragmatism. Just as "because I like it" does not qualify as a valid criterion for the doctrine of the Church, it is likewise not a valid criterion for evaluating music for the sacred liturgy. Liturgical music may certainly evoke our emotions, but it must not be overly sentimental. Liturgical art, if it aims to be universal, must rise above sentimentality to a beauty that can be perceived both by those who are highly educated and by those who do not have a refined ear.

## *Liturgical Discomfort*

*In some cases, a parish priest might fully agree with this analysis but encounter conflict with his musicians regarding the appropriateness of their musical choices. The musicians might defend their choices on the basis of approval from a previous priest, while the new priest has different opinions. How should such situations be handled, especially considering varying tastes and discernments of the artistic quality of music?*

Differentiating between what is truly sacred and artistically beautiful and what merely caters to the personal preferences of an individual person or congregation is a difficult task. Bishops' conferences have sometimes provided pastoral guidelines for the sacred music in parishes, but on the ground

[10] Benedict XVI, *New Song*, 136.

level these decisions are the responsibility of the pastor, who is ultimately responsible for the liturgical celebrations at his parish. Where there exists the possibility of music directors and music staff, these decisions are often delegated, as oftentimes, the music director has a more thorough training and understanding of sacred music than the pastor, who may have received only rudimentary training in sacred music. In these cases, the music director must work with the pastor and advise him as he is able, though he ultimately remains under his authority, as he is the pastor of the flock.

*However, if priests and bishops prioritize utility, by seeking to attract and keep a congregation engaged without upsetting them and challenging them, devout men and women may find themselves trapped in a situation where the liturgy and its music becomes all about people and their feelings rather than about God and his holiness. Sometimes, there appears to be an emphasis on whether the music evokes positive or negative emotions in people, reflecting a consumerism-driven approach that evaluates the liturgy and liturgical music primarily on the basis of collected data about people's personal experiences. How do you believe this impacts our understanding of and encounter with the liturgy, when the music becomes more about seeking to elicit positive emotions in people rather than offering the best of ourselves for the worship of God?*

The essence of the liturgy is to confront and transform; it is about engaging with the very mystery of God. Consequently, sometimes the liturgy *should* make us uncomfortable. That discomfort can jolt us out of our complacency and lead us to a conversion of life, much like Saint Paul on his journey to Damascus. There is a real danger in reducing the liturgy to a mere feel-good experience, as if the Church were offering a spiritual palliative on Sunday mornings. To view

Christianity as a panacea inoculates us against the idea that we must convert our lives. If we were discussing preaching instead of music, we might ask how many sermons would mention challenging doctrines, such as the reality of hell, or the necessity of following the moral teachings of the Church even when commonly ignored and misrepresented in society. How many homilies truly emphasize the call to conversion and transformation of life, rather than simply reassuring us that God loves us without any implications for our actions?

The liturgy is a sacred space where we encounter the realities of our faith, including those that are uncomfortable or challenging. If we respond maturely, we will thank God for these opportunities to grow in our faith. However, we must bear misunderstanding with patience, not changing the liturgy to adapt to worldly perspectives, but rather, educating and forming all those who are honestly seeking to engage with the Church's liturgical tradition but who may have some difficulty with understanding it and participating in it.

## *Liturgical Sacred Music and Nonliturgical Religious Music*

*The term "sacred music" is commonly understood as an umbrella term that can include many different styles of religious music that may or may not be "liturgical music" but include religious themes and texts, such as the musical genre of the oratorio (for example, Handel's* Messiah*). Can you speak to this distinction between liturgical music and religious music that may be sacred in its theme but is not inherently liturgical?*

Certainly, music with clear liturgical origins is easily identifiable as suitable for worship. When we consider the Gregorian chant introit of Easter Day, "Resurrexi", or that of

Christmas Day, "Puer natus est nobis", it is unimaginable that these were created for any purpose or context other than the liturgy. Their contemplative tones serve to transport the congregation into a mystical experience—to partake in the heavenly liturgy, to harmonize with the choir of angels and saints who stand before the Throne and the Lamb, holding harps and golden bowls filled with incense, singing a new song (see Rev 5:6–9). However, alongside Gregorian chant, there are of course many other styles and genres of sacred music. Some choral and orchestral music that had been composed specifically for the liturgy has largely been set aside since the time of Saint Pius X because of its length and decadent musical expression. There are also styles of religious music that are not liturgical in their essence or intention, but can be considered appropriate for devotional use or for private prayer. Similarly, symphonies or solo instrumental works, originally intended for the concert hall, might contain religious elements but are incompatible with the liturgy because of their musical form or inclusion of profane elements.

In contemporary times, discerning music suitable for the liturgy can be challenging, sometimes unfortunately resulting in an anarchical free-for-all in selecting the music for the liturgy. On one hand, there is a need to embrace and respect the legitimate expressions and desires of the people; and on the other hand, there is an essential responsibility not to oppose the liturgy and its essence. This raises questions: Should we prohibit the performance of a slow movement from a Vivaldi or Bach concerto during the offertory or distribution of Communion, even if it was not originally composed for the liturgy, but possesses extraordinary beauty that reflects divine beauty? Cannot such works be deemed an "incarnation" of the Beautiful and employed in the liturgy where they are appropriate and do not draw undue attention to themselves by inordinately lengthening the liturgical celebration? Or, another question: Should some forms of truly sacred music that are difficult, such as polyphony, be replaced by music of perhaps lesser quality because it is more practical or immediately accessible to the choir or congregation?

Some of these questions may have different answers depending on the unique circumstances in which they are asked, but the decisions must always be guided by the principles laid out in the Church's liturgical documents and made with a deep understanding of the nature and purpose of sacred music. Regardless of how the principles are applied, we must strive to maintain the integrity of the liturgy and recognize that the potential for beauty and spiritual edification exists within a diversity of musical expressions.

## *The Living Tradition of Sacred Music*

*As Paul writes in his letter to the Philippians, "Whatever is true, whatever is honorable, whatever is just, whatever is pure, whatever is lovely, whatever is gracious, if there is any excellence, if there is anything worthy of praise, think about these things"(4:8). In light of this exhortation, how can church musicians and composers today ensure that their musical selections and compositions align with the tradition of truly sacred art, rather than creating everything anew and starting a musical tradition from scratch?*

We face a significant challenge today in integrating the richness of our sacred musical tradition with contemporary forms and musical expressions. The selection of music for the liturgy must be approached with a profound sense of reverence and humility. Our choices should reflect not our personal preferences, but our discernment of what most suitably glorifies God and enriches the spirit of the liturgy. It is not merely a matter of personal taste, but an offering of our best—the "first fruits"—to God. We must remember that what we offer in the liturgy must be akin to Abel's sacrifice, a pure and worthy gift to the Lord of the first fruits of our flock.

Throughout history, the role of great composers has been to enhance the liturgical texts, transforming them into grand works of art. They built upon tradition, sometimes expanding its boundaries and musical limits, but always remaining rooted in the Church's rich musical heritage. These composers did not merely create artful music; they offered a medium through which the liturgy could speak more profoundly to the hearts of the faithful through their unique musical imagination and creativity. According to the logic of the Incarnation, it is God Himself, the Divine Artist, who illuminates man to create together with Him. What Pope Saint John Paul II wrote concerning sacred art is also true of sacred music, that it is in a certain sense a sacrament, "by analogy with what occurs in the sacraments . . . [making] present the mystery of the Incarnation in one or other of its aspects."[11]

Pope Benedict XVI possessed a clear vision for the continued development of sacred music and the liturgy, allowing the older liturgical rites to grow and inform, emphasizing mutual enrichment between the old and the new. Many priests have shared that in celebrating the older form of the Mass, what Pope Benedict called the Extraordinary Form, they have rediscovered how to celebrate properly the current Roman Missal that Pope Benedict termed the Ordinary Form. Oftentimes, this reconnection with the older

[11] Pope John Paul II, Letter to Artists (April 4, 1999), no. 8.

liturgical traditions of the Church has led to a reconnection and even a flourishing of the musical tradition of the Church in the process.

However, regardless of the form of the liturgy that is celebrated, the essence of sacred music should remain the same: an offering of the best of man, rooted in the living tradition and oriented toward the glorification of God and the sanctification of the faithful. By keeping these principles at the forefront of our minds, we can ensure that the sacred music composed and offered in the liturgy remains true to the Church's tradition while also being open to the inspiration of the Holy Spirit in our own time. In this way, we can continue to enrich the Church's musical tradition, offering our unique gifts to God and drawing the faithful ever deeper into the mystery of His divine life.

3

# THE POWER OF GREGORIAN CHANT

## *From African Village to Universal Church: The Unity of Sacred Music*

PETER CARTER: *Your Eminence, you've mentioned that when growing up, the music in the liturgies was only permitted to be in Latin and in French, not the local vernacular languages of Guinea. Was the Sunday Mass at the village parish a sung Mass?*

ROBERT CARDINAL SARAH: Yes, the French missionaries who brought the faith to our village taught us primarily Gregorian chant and French hymns. Parts of the Mass were chanted in Latin, such as the introit, the Gloria, and the Credo, with some French hymns as well, very similar to how the missionaries celebrated Mass in France. On Sundays, we would also have sung Vespers and Benediction, which many families would attend in addition to the morning Mass. During Benediction, we would sing the Latin hymns of Saint Thomas Aquinas such as "Adoro te devote", "O Salutaris Hostia", and "Tantum Ergo".

*Did the people of your village understand Latin?*

Not well, but they were able to learn the Latin texts of the ordinary of the Mass since these texts were repeated at every Mass. Everyone knew and sang the Kyrie, Gloria, Credo III, Sanctus, and Agnus Dei, for example.

*In my experience as a church musician, I have encountered many people, including priests, who seem rather averse to Gregorian chant or even Latin in general, believing that they are either inaccessible or no longer relevant after the Second Vatican Council. Some priests seem to hesitate to use the Latin chants of the Mass, concerned that the laity may lack understanding of the words they are singing and therefore limit their participation in the liturgy. Do you think that singing in Latin was a barrier to liturgical participation in your village growing up?*

No, not at all. The people of my village were able to participate in the sacred liturgy with great faith, and sacred music played a significant role in facilitating this participation. We would learn and listen to the Word of God and the Gospels translated into our native language, but when we sang in Church, it was either in Latin or French. This felt normal and didn't pose any barrier or problem for us. Learning to sing the parts of the Mass was an integral aspect of our religious instruction, so singing in Latin was a natural for us in our experience of Christian worship.

To provide some additional context, Guinea is a linguistically diverse country with around eight common languages but over forty different local languages. During my childhood, approximately 75 percent of the Guinean population was Muslim, and they chanted exclusively in Arabic. When we, as Christians, sang in Latin or French, it was perceived as a distinctly Christian practice. Having a shared sacred language was and remains crucial for uniting and strengthening the bond among Guinean Catholics. Latin is essential to our identity, as we are part of the Latin Church, so I don't believe it was wrong in any way for us to learn to sing in Latin and French. It made sense that in becoming Christian, we needed to learn to sing the music of the Church.

After the Second Vatican Council, the Church in Guinea began to incorporate African styles of music and African instruments into the liturgy, but this was not the case during my upbringing. Today, in many places in Africa, only African music is used. Sometimes, the Credo or Gloria is still chanted in Latin, but the majority of the music is African.

*Do you think that something is lost if people only know and sing music from their own local culture and only in their vernacular languages, whether in Africa or anywhere else?*

Yes, I believe that if we limit ourselves to singing music only in our native language, we risk isolating ourselves from the broader tradition of the Church and confining our worship to our local culture. When we sing in the sacred language of the Church, such as chanting the Credo in Latin, our focus shifts from ourselves to the universal Christian tradition and the universal Church family. If we lose Latin then we lose a sense of the universality and shared liturgical culture that binds the Church together. Pope Saint John XXIII eloquently expressed the importance of Latin as the Church's language in his apostolic constitution *Veterum sapientia*: "Of its very nature Latin is most suitable for promoting every form of culture among peoples. It gives rise to no jealousies. It does not favor any one nation, but presents itself with equal impartiality to all and is equally acceptable to all."[1]

In the same document, Saint John XXIII quotes Pope Pius XI, emphasizing that the Church, due to its universal nature and enduring mission, requires a language that is "universal, immutable, and non-vernacular".[2] It is truly regrettable

[1] John XXIII, apostolic constitution *Veterum sapientia* (On the Promotion of the Study of Latin) (February 22, 1962).

[2] Ibid., quoting Pius XI, *Epist. Ap. Officiorum omnium*, Aug. 1, 1922: AAS 14 (1922), 452.

if we "cancel" our history and tradition, attempting to start everything anew. The Church is like a living tree, and if we cut ourselves off from our roots then the tree will wither and die. Or, to use another analogy, we are like a large stream, but if we cut ourselves off from our wellspring, we will dry up and die out. To be fully alive and thrive, we must know and celebrate our tradition and maintain continuity with it.

## *The Model of Sacred Music*

*Saint Pius X described Gregorian chant as the "supreme model for sacred music". In what way does Gregorian chant uniquely embody Pope Saint Pius X's criteria for sacred music: sanctity, beauty, and universality?*

In *Tra le sollecitudini*, right after Saint Pius X lists the *sine qua non* criteria of sacred music—sanctity, goodness of form, and universality—he states:

> These qualities are to be found, in the highest degree, in Gregorian Chant, which is, consequently the Chant proper to the Roman Church, the only chant she has inherited from the ancient fathers, which she has jealously guarded for centuries in her liturgical codices, which she directly proposes to the faithful as her own, which she prescribes exclusively for some parts of the liturgy, and which the most recent studies have so happily restored to their integrity and purity.[3]

The universality of Gregorian chant in the past can be compared to the role of English as a global lingua franca today. People of all races, beliefs, ages, and cultures can communicate instantly when a conversation begins in the nearly universal spoken language of Shakespeare. However, view-

[3] Pope Pius X, motu proprio *Tra le sollecitudini* (On Sacred Music) (November 22, 1903), no. 3, https://adoremus.org/1903/11/tra-le-sollecitudini/.

ing Gregorian chant and the Latin language solely through this lens would be reductionist and misleading. Gregorian chant, born primarily of Latin and some Greek, is a small but magnificent artistic miracle. Just as a beautiful symphony without words can move us to tears, or a song in a foreign language can evoke indescribable emotions, Gregorian chant takes us "where it wants to go" rather than where we desire, provided we truly open ourselves to it and wish to understand its musical meaning. Prayer moves us in this way as well. We need only recall Saint Paul's words regarding authentic prayer as being "God praying within us": "Likewise the Spirit helps us in our weakness; for we do not know how to pray as we ought, but the Spirit himself intercedes for us with sighs too deep for words. And he who searches the hearts of men knows what is the mind of the Spirit, because the Spirit intercedes for the saints according to the will of God" (Rom 8:26–27). Those who pray with Gregorian chant pray to God, but God also prays within them. This is the source of the chant's universality and its suitability for the entire people of God. Pope Saint John Paul II eloquently describes this universality: "Gregorian chant, with its inspired modulations, was to become down the centuries the music of the Church's faith in the liturgical celebration of the sacred mysteries. The 'beautiful' was thus wedded to the 'true', so that through art too souls might be lifted up from the world of the senses to the eternal."[4] Through this music, which itself is prayer, God visits us, and we go to meet Him. Pope Benedict articulates this encounter with God who has made Himself known through music:

> The Holy Spirit, who had inspired David to sing and to pray, moves him to speak of Christ, indeed causes him to

[4] Pope John Paul II, Letter of His Holiness Pope John Paul II to Artists (April 4, 1999), no. 7.

become the very mouth of Christ, thus enabling us in the Psalms to speak through Christ, in the Holy Spirit, to the Father. Now this exegesis of the Psalms, at once christological and pneumatological, not only concerns the text but also includes the element of music. It is the Holy Spirit who teaches us to sing—first David and then, through him, Israel and the Church. Yes, singing, the surpassing of ordinary speech, is a "pneumatic" event. Church music comes into being as a "charism", a gift of the Spirit. It is the true *glossolalia*, the new tongue that comes from the Holy Spirit. It is above all in Church music that the "sober inebriation" of faith takes place—an inebriation surpassing all the possibilities of mere rationality. But this intoxication remains sober, because Christ and the Holy Spirit belong together, because this drunken speech stays totally within the discipline of the Logos, in a new rationality that, beyond all words, serves the primordial Word, the ground of all reason.[5]

## *A Journey to Faith Through Gregorian Chant*

ROBERT CARDINAL SARAH: André Charlier, a renowned French jazz composer and drummer, offers a powerful testimony to the transformative nature of Gregorian chant. His journey from being a nonbeliever to becoming a Christian was influenced by his encounter with this sacred music. Charlier shares his story:

> The Gregorian chant that I discovered before becoming a Christian, before having faith, revealed to me things that were not of this earth and that no other human music, even if it were brilliant, could express. Thus, I discovered the love of Christ, better than in many sermons, in the antiphon "Ubi Caritas et Amor." This ineffable mystery of

[5] Joseph Cardinal Ratzinger, *The Spirit of the Liturgy* (Ignatius Press, 2000), p. 140.

> redemption, the mystery of a sacrificed God who is the savior of His people, I unveiled by hearing a monastic choir sing during Holy Week the "Christus Factus Est". . . . In short, Gregorian chant took me much further than human music; it made me glimpse the reality of these mysteries that I did not suspect.[6]

Charlier's background in modern jazz, a genre often associated with improvisation, syncopation, and complex harmonies, makes his insights into the sacred nature of Gregorian chant all the more striking. His testimony is a powerful reminder that Gregorian chant, with its spiritual roots in divine inspiration, has the capacity to touch the hearts of even those who are not initially drawn to religious faith. When listening to Gregorian chant, one can immediately sense that this music stems from an encounter with God. It is not merely a song, but a sung meditation, a musical contemplation of God. Through Gregorian chant, the angels themselves seem to communicate the heavenly liturgy to us. It is inspired and inspiring, religious and divine—truly sacred music. Unlike secular music, even the jazz that Charlier was accustomed to, which can often be genuinely fun and exciting, and sometimes even noisy, Gregorian chant is devoid of these superficial qualities. Its simplicity and purity of form and expression makes it capable of revealing God's presence, gently touching and sometimes even piercing the heart. The key difference between Gregorian chant and contemporary secular music is that Gregorian chant is a sung contemplation of God's glory, originating from God through the inspiration of the Holy Spirit. It is music that personally helps me connect with God, music that God listens to as coming from the heart. Simone Weil beautifully describes how

[6] Henri Charlier and André Charlier, *Le Chant grégorien* (Martin Morin, 1967), 12.

Gregorian chant nourishes our faith and serves as a form of contemplation:

> When we listen to Bach or to a Gregorian melody, all the faculties of the soul become tense and silent in order to apprehend this thing of perfect beauty, each after its own fashion. The intelligence among the rest: it finds nothing in this thing it hears to affirm or deny, but it feeds upon it.
>
> Should not faith be an adherence of this kind?
>
> The mysteries of faith are degraded if they are made into an object of affirmation and negation, when in reality they should be an object of contemplation.[7]

With all these things in mind, it is entirely understandable why the Second Vatican Council affirmed Gregorian chant as the proper chant of the Roman liturgy, giving it principal place in liturgical actions.[8] Gregorian chant is unparalleled in its beauty and its ability to lead us to the mystery of God.

## *The Encounter with the Living God*

*God has called many of His saints to serve the Church through their specific charisms, and we often refer to their followers as adopting their way of prayer, their spirituality (for example, Franciscan spirituality, Dominican spirituality, Jesuit spirituality). However, since the liturgy is meant for the entire body of Christ and not just certain members, could we say that the liturgy is, in a sense, the spirituality of the Church? And should the Roman liturgy and its music, Gregorian chant, thus be an integral part of the spirituality of all Christians belonging to the Roman Rite?*

[7] Simone Weil, *Gravity and Grace*, trans. Arthur Wills (G.P. Putnam's Sons, 1952), 183.

[8] Vatican Council II, Constitution on the Sacred Liturgy *Sacrosanctum concilium* (December 4, 1963), no. 116.

Gregorian chant can be rightfully regarded as a "necessary and integral part of the solemn Liturgy" and the authentic chant of the Church, as *Sacrosanctum concilium* declares.[9] However, it is not merely an expression of a distinct spirituality, like the different charisms of religious orders. As genuine liturgical chant, it is the embodiment of the Logos, which is why it holds universal significance. Pope Benedict spoke of this epiphany of the Logos in the liturgy:

> "The Word became flesh and lived [pitched his tent] among us, and we have seen his glory" (John 1:14). The "Word" to which Christian worship refers is first of all not a text, but a living reality: a God who is self-communicating meaning and who communicates himself by becoming a human being. This incarnation is the sacred tent, the focal point of all worship which looks at the glory of God and gives him honor.[10]

The liturgy, more than just the spirituality of the Church, reflects and serves as a repository for the various spiritualities and charisms that adorn and enrich the Church. In the liturgy, the Church encounters Christ truly present in the sacrament of His Body and Blood, but also through sacred images and sacred music, which manifest His presence to us. Outside of the liturgy, God reveals Himself to us and to the world in unique and diverse spiritualities and charisms. But in the liturgy, all Christians are united by participating in the sacraments that Christ instituted for the salvation of His spouse, the Church.

[9] Ibid., nos. 112, 116.

[10] Pope Benedict XVI (Joseph Ratzinger), "Sing Artistically for God", in *A New Song for the Lord: Faith in Christ and Liturgy Today* (Crossroad Publishing Company, 2013), 153.

## *Learning to Love the Church's Musical Tradition*

*What advice do you have for those who may not have an appreciation for the Church's tradition of liturgical music, and who perhaps even possess a dislike for Gregorian chant?*

Familiarity often plays a significant role in shaping our personal preferences. Whenever we experience something foreign, it can take time to acclimate ourselves to understand it before we can learn to appreciate it deeply. It is often easier to disengage from what we do not understand and to conclude quickly that we do not like something than to give the time and energy needed to be fully engaged with it. We must have a certain humility toward that which we do not understand and a patience with ourselves and with the process of becoming familiar with and learning to appreciate whatever is considered good, though unfamiliar and foreign. This is all the more important when it comes to everything surrounding the most important thing in our lives, our encounter with Christ, both within and outside of the liturgy.

When my own parents converted to the Catholic Church, they had a great many things to learn that were undoubtedly foreign to them, most especially how the Christian ought to pray. However, over time, the liturgy and the Gregorian chants they learned to sing became part of their identity as Christians, coming to find them as truly beautiful and deeply moving.

One of the problems is that many Christians today have never been exposed to Gregorian chant and therefore do not have any appreciation for it. This disconnect between our rich musical and liturgical tradition and the common experience of the liturgy is a great loss, causing a separation from the musical tradition that has been shared over the centuries by many of the saints who came before us. This highlights the importance of education for appreciating sacred music and understanding its purpose as a way to reach God. If we have grown accustomed to secular styles of music in the liturgy, Gregorian chant and other forms of true sacred music may sound cold or distant to us. However, this very quality allows our passions to be calmed, enabling us to see the Holy Mass with the eyes of faith and live it as Christ, the Apostles, and centuries of the Church's tradition have lived it. When one seeks God and enters the "language" of the sacred, initial unfamiliarity and even dislike can melt away and transform into love. Conversely, if we obstinately persist in our own ways, personal ideas of how things should be, or preferred styles of music, then our encounter with the sacred may even cause us to react with disgust. We must not hold our preferences and personal experiences too obstinately, whether they are ignorant or refined, if doing so allows them to stand between us and our participation in the divine mysteries.

To the faithful who do not know or appreciate the music of the Church's tradition, I would recommend, above all, being patient and diligent in faith. Indeed, it is always faith that leads to the mystery of God—"without faith, it is impossible to please him" (Heb 11:6). By recognizing the beauty present in sacred music, one can open one's heart to the light of the Spirit. This purifying contemplation of God, looking at God and allowing His light to shine on us, should be our chief prayer in the Mass. As Christ said, "Blessed are the pure in heart, for they shall see God" (Mt 5:8).

# Part II

# Contemplation and Actual Participation

# 4

# *PARTICIPATIO ACTUOSA* AND CONGREGATIONAL SINGING

PETER CARTER: *One element of the liturgical movement of the twentieth century was to suggest congregational singing as a form of participation in the liturgy. Pope Saint Pius X specifically mentions this in his 1903 motu proprio* Tra le sollecitudini *when he writes, "Special efforts are to be made to restore the use of the Gregorian Chant by the people, so that the faithful may again take a more active part in the ecclesiastical offices, as was the case in ancient times."*[1] *Can you elaborate on the significance of the phrase "participatio actuosa" used by Pope Saint Pius X?*

ROBERT CARDINAL SARAH: This phrase, which was first introduced by Pope Saint Pius X, became one of the chief principles of the liturgical reforms of the 1960s, especially as expounded upon in the Second Vatican Council's document on the sacred liturgy, *Sacrosanctum concilium*, and the following Instruction on Music in the Liturgy, *Musicam sacram*, in 1967. As Cardinal Ratzinger noted in 1978, "One of the guiding words of the conciliar liturgical reform was rightly participatio actuosa, the 'active' or 'actual' participation of the entire 'people of God' in the liturgy."[2] However, debate

[1] Pius X, motu proprio *Tra le sollecitudini* (On Sacred Music) (November 22, 1903), no. 3, https://adoremus.org/1903/11/tra-le-sollecitudini/.

[2] Joseph Ratzinger (Benedict XVI), *Lodate Dio con arte* (Marcianum Press, 2011), 45–46.

has arisen over the interpretation and application of "active" versus "actual" participation within the liturgy. The subtle differences in connotation between these translations lie at the heart of the ongoing debate.

*What was the original purpose of making "actual participation" one of the main criteria of liturgical reform?*

The commitment of the Council Fathers to integrate the participation of the faithful in liturgical celebrations, especially in the Holy Mass, came from a desire to renew the Church with holiness and apostolic fervor, especially through the renewal of the liturgy. As stated in *Sacrosanctum concilium*: "The Church, therefore, earnestly desires that Christ's faithful, when present at this mystery of faith, should not be there as strangers or silent spectators; on the contrary, through a good understanding of the rites and prayers they should take part in the sacred action conscious of what they are doing, with devotion and full collaboration."[3] Liturgical rites are celebrations of the entire Church, the holy people gathered under the guidance of the priest or bishop. The priest offers the Sacrifice of the Mass in the person of Christ, and he and his assisting ministers—deacons, altar servers, readers, commentators, and the Schola Cantorum or lay choir—each have a special role according to their unique office and function. When the priest prays, he does so on behalf of the entire Church. The same is true for when the Scriptures are read and when the choir sings. Thus, the faithful attending should listen to these prayers with reverence and participate vocally in the responses and music that belong to them.

[3] Vatican Council II, Constitution on the Sacred Liturgy *Sacrosanctum concilium* (December 4, 1963), no. 48.

The choir, also known as the Schola Cantorum, has historically sung much of the music of the Mass that was often too complex to be sung by the entire congregation. Pope Saint Pius X, in *Tra le sollecitudini*, envisioned the restoration of the Schola Cantorum:

> Let care be taken to restore, at least in the principal churches, the ancient *Scholae Cantorum*, as has been done with excellent fruit in a great many places. It is not difficult for a zealous clergy to institute such Scholae even in smaller churches and country parishes—nay, in these last the pastors will find a very easy means of gathering around them both children and adults, to their own profit and the edification of the people.[4]

The call for the active participation of the faithful does not diminish the unique role of the Schola Cantorum with their distinct musical repertoire. The post-conciliar emphasis on congregational singing was not intended to replace the Schola Cantorum's original function, which is especially important given the near abandonment of Gregorian chant and sacred polyphony in many places. Rather, the Church understands that the active participation of the faithful may be expressed both by silence and listening, as when the Schola Cantorum sings alone or during the prayers of the priest, and when the whole assembly is actively involved with singing, such as for the Kyrie and Gloria. The music of the congregation and that of the Schola Cantorum are complementary, rather than one being preferred to the exclusion of the other. One need only look to the papal liturgies to understand how the Church wishes this teaching to be understood in practice.

[4] *Tra le sollecitudini*, no. 27.

I also fondly recall a Mass at Saint-Eustache in Paris that beautifully exemplified this balance: The organ played before and after the celebration of Mass, the choir led the assembly in song, and Gregorian chant and polyphony were sung by the choir.

## *Contradictory Interpretations of* Sacrosanctum concilium

*It seems that today there still exists a great deal of misunderstanding surrounding the liturgical directives of* Sacrosanctum concilium, *the Constitution on the Sacred Liturgy of the Second Vatican Council, with some contradictory interpretations of how they should be implemented.*

The heart of the issue, and the surrounding confusion, lies in the interpretation of three articles in the document. Article 28 states: "In liturgical celebrations, each person, minister or layman, who has an office to perform, should do all of, but only, those parts which pertain to his office by the nature of the rite and the principles of liturgy."[5] This suggests a distinction between the roles of the clergy, the choir, and the congregation. Article 30, on the other hand, encourages the active participation of the people through various means, including singing, while also mentioning the importance of reverent silence at the proper times: "To promote active participation, the people should be encouraged to take part by means of acclamations, responses, psalmody, antiphons, and songs, as well as by actions, gestures, and bodily attitudes. And at the proper times all should observe a reverent silence."[6] Ratzinger notes that the language of these articles

[5] *Sacrosanctum concilium*, no. 28.

[6] Ibid., no. 30.

"may have lent themselves to such restrictions, basing participation itself, to a large extent, on external actions".[7]

When we come to article 114, the tension becomes more evident. The article stresses that "The treasure of sacred music is to be preserved and fostered with great care. Choirs must be diligently promoted, especially in cathedral churches."[8] At the same time, it calls for the active participation of the entire assembly in every liturgical service that involves singing, in keeping with articles 28 and 30.

*The resurgence of congregational singing in many places after Vatican II has oftentimes led to the exclusion of any choral music in the liturgy that is noncongregational. If, as some priests and bishops suggest, the "active participation of the people" means that all of the liturgical music must be congregational, then how can the heritage of sacred music be preserved and cultivated when much of this music is not possible for the congregation to sing, but only for trained choral singers?*

The key to resolving this apparent conflict lies in understanding that "active participation" does not necessarily mean that everyone must sing everything at all times. Rather, it means that the congregation should be engaged in the liturgy, whether through singing, listening, or silent prayer. Cardinal Ratzinger offers a profound insight into this matter. Here we must quote him at length to resolve the tension:

> The impression arose that active participation only existed where there was verifiable external activity: speeches, songs, sermons, liturgical assistance. Articles 28 and 30 of the liturgical Constitution, which define active participation,

[7] Benedict XVI, *Lodate Dio*, 45–46.

[8] *Sacrosanctum concilium*, no. 114.

> may have lent themselves to such restrictions, basing participation itself, to a large extent, on external actions. Nevertheless, it is also remembered there how participatio actuosa includes silence. In connection with this, one must ask: why should only speaking and not also listening, perceiving with the senses and with the spirit, constitute active spiritual participation? Are perceiving, grasping, and being moved not active? Is there not also a diminishment of man here, who is reduced to mere oral expression, although today we all know that what emerges in us in a rationally conscious manner on the surface is only the tip of an iceberg with respect to the whole of man? Let us be even more concrete: now, quite a few people can sing better "with the heart" than "with the mouth", but to them the singing of those who can sing with the mouth can truly make their hearts sing, so that they sing, so to speak, even in those people, and both grateful listening and the performance of the singers become together a single praise to God. Should we absolutely force those who cannot sing to sing, thus silencing their hearts and those of others? This says nothing against the singing of the entire people of the faithful, which maintains its function unaltered in the church, but it says everything against an exclusivity that cannot be justified by tradition or by the thing itself.[9]

The rendering of *actuosa* as "active" participation rather than "actual" participation has led many to assume that the faithful must be constantly *doing something*. This misconception reduces participation to mere physical activity and visible engagement. But this understanding is incomplete and fails to capture the essence of what Vatican II means by actual participation. Some examples of "active" participation today can be likened to singing "Happy Birthday" at a birthday party, which may be a communal activity but lacks the

[9] Benedict XVI, *Lodate Dio*, 45–46.

sacredness and solemnity proper to the spirit of the liturgy. While the Church has encouraged greater involvement of the faithful in the liturgy, we must ensure that this openness does not compromise the profound meaning of actual participation in the sacred mysteries.

As we can see, "active" participation must be understood as encompassing both external and internal dimensions, and that attentive and prayerful listening can be just as much a form of participation as singing. We must avoid any idea of participation that forces everyone either to be "silent spectators" or, conversely, to sing at all times, thereby excluding those who participate most deeply through prayerful silence. Article 114, then, must be understood as calling for a balance between the preservation of the Church's musical heritage through the Schola Cantorum and the singing of the entire assembly in the liturgy. The Schola Cantorum can sing alone for the more complex choral music and also lead the congregation in singing the simpler chants, responses, and acclamations. When the choir sings alone, the congregation rightly participates through active listening and silent prayer. This approach toward active participation is truly in harmony with the Council's vision of a liturgy in which all the faithful, choir, and clergy are engaged, each in their own proper way. Actual participation means entering deeply, with faith and loving presence, into the sacred mystery being celebrated. It is dying with Christ, suffering with Him in silence—not simply doing something. The congregation's role is more akin to that of Saint John and the Virgin Mary, who participated in Jesus' death on the cross through silent, loving presence. While the priest, cantor, or choir perform their distinctive roles in the liturgy, the people join Christ not by dancing or crying out but by silent unity with His sacrifice.

I witnessed this myself as a child, seeing my parents participating profoundly in the liturgy through silent contemplation, and they grew and were strengthened in their faith as a result. Without faith, there is no true liturgical participation. One can outwardly follow rituals out of duty, but only faith enables full entry into the mystery of Christ who dies for us. It is not about keeping everyone busy with activities. Rather, it means that we become, little by little, Christ Himself. Then, after Mass, people will see Christ living in us—in how we speak, act, and serve. This is what it means to be a Christian. In other words, it is to be able to say with Saint Paul: "I have been crucified with Christ; it is no longer I who live, but Christ who lives in me; and the life I now live in the flesh I live by faith in the Son of God, who loved me and gave himself for me" (Gal 2:20).

The 1967 document *Musicam sacram* provides more specific guidance on achieving this balance, discussing the prioritization of certain Mass parts for congregational singing while allowing the choir to take on more complex musical settings. It also cautions against completely excluding the people from the proper and ordinary parts of the Mass, but also acknowledges that some parts may be sung by the choir alone, especially if the faithful have not yet been sufficiently instructed or if polyphonic musical settings are used. This approach is not a novel invention; in the sixth century, Saint Benedict of Nursia understood this well, commanding his monks not to allow anyone to read or sing unless they could, in doing so, "give edification to the hearers".[10]

[10] Saint Benedict, *The Rule of St. Benedict*, trans. Justin McCann (Sheed & Ward, 1976), 61.

*What is the specific guidance that* Musicam sacram *gives us for understanding "active participation" in the liturgy?*

Following the Second Vatican Council, the Sacred Congregation of Rites issued *Musicam sacram* in 1967, clarifying how actual participation in the liturgy should be understood. Paragraph 15 of *Musicam sacram* states:

> The faithful fulfill their liturgical role by making that full, conscious and active participation which is demanded by the nature of the liturgy itself and which is, by reason of baptism, the right and duty of the Christian people. This participation
>
> (a) Should be above all internal, in the sense that by it the faithful join their mind to what they pronounce or hear, and cooperate with heavenly grace,
>
> (b) Must be, on the other hand, external also, that is, such as to show the internal participation by gestures and bodily attitudes, by the acclamations, responses and singing.
>
> The faithful should also be taught to unite themselves interiorly to what the ministers or choir sing, so that by listening to them they may raise their minds to God.[11]

## *A Balance of Musical Roles*

*In papal liturgies, we see Gregorian chant and polyphony sung by the Sistine Chapel Choir, and parts of the Mass sung by the congregation, including simple settings of parts of the Mass ordinary, such as the Kyrie, and a few of the Mass propers, such as the responsorial psalm and Alleluia. Yet, in most parishes, the role of the*

[11] Vatican Council II, Instruction on Music in the Liturgy *Musicam sacram* (March 5, 1967), no. 15.

*choir is primarily to serve as an aid to congregational singing, rather than having a distinct musical role in singing noncongregational settings of the propers, historically sung to Latin Gregorian chant, and polyphonic settings of parts of the Mass ordinary, such as the Kyrie, Gloria, Sanctus, and Agnus Dei. Oftentimes, rather than seeking the balance exemplified in the papal liturgies, there exists in many parishes a tension between the congregational music and the noncongregational choral music that forms the majority of the "treasury of sacred music" that Vatican II said should be "preserved and fostered with great care".*[12] *Why do you think this tension exists?*

Allow me to clarify some of these terms in case readers may have difficulty in understanding your question: The "Mass propers" are chants that change from one Mass to another—they are proper or unique to certain days and feasts of the liturgical year. The Mass propers sometimes vary but usually include an entrance antiphon (historically called the "introit"), responsorial psalm (historically the gradual), Gospel acclamation (historically the Alleluia or tract), offertory antiphon, and Communion antiphon. The "Mass ordinary" refers to those texts of the Mass that remain the same from one celebration of Mass to another—they are the texts that are ordinarily prayed and sung. The texts also sometimes vary, but Sunday Masses include the Kyrie, Gloria, Credo, Sanctus, memorial acclamation, Our Father, and Agnus Dei.

To answer your question, it is certainly true that in the post-conciliar liturgical movement there is a clear emphasis on congregational song, even when it has resulted in sometimes taking away some of the music that was formerly sung only by the choir. This was typically perceived as an effort

[12] *Sacrosanctum concilium*, no. 14.

to implement the Council's desire that the faithful "should not be there as strangers or silent spectators" but "should take part in the sacred action conscious of what they are doing, with devotion and full collaboration".[13] One clear example of this is the formation of the responsorial psalm in the Novus Ordo Missae which usually takes the place of the gradual chant, which when sung, is sung only by the choir. However, it is important to note that the singing of the gradual chant remains a valid option in the missal of Paul VI and is still commonly sung in monasteries, such as the monastery of Solesmes in France. This is an example of how the Church permits a diversity of options so that local parishes and communities can choose the option that is appropriate for their particular circumstances.

However, it is not that the faithful "have a right" to sing the responsorial psalm that is then unjustly taken away if the choir instead sings the Gregorian setting of the gradual or a choral setting of the psalm. If, as your question suggests, parishes insist on one musical form to the complete exclusion of the possibility of the other valid options, then we have lost sight of what the liturgy is and the role of liturgical music. It is primarily about the praise and worship of almighty God, and through that praise we become edified and sanctified.

I think Pope Benedict's words in regard to the pre-conciliar form of the Mass could be understood with regard to the Church's tradition of sacred music more broadly, whether applying them to the gradual specifically or to the polyphonic masterworks of the Church's musical tradition more generally: "What earlier generations held as sacred, remains

[13] Ibid., no. 48.

sacred and great for us too, and it cannot be all of a sudden entirely forbidden or even considered harmful. It behooves all of us to preserve the riches which have developed in the Church's faith and prayer, and to give them their proper place."[14]

The Church allows for some of the antiphons of the Mass to be replaced by other legitimate forms of sacred music during the entrance, offertory, and Communion. However, the Church presents the singing of liturgical texts of these propers as the primary option for choosing music that is appropriate for liturgical celebrations. If we choose to sing any kind of song as long as the congregation is singing, then we lose the essence of what we are celebrating in the liturgy, which is especially conveyed through the text of the Mass propers that the Church has already chosen as specifically appropriate for the liturgy. And although the congregation's participation should not be that of "silent spectators", it does also not primarily consist of congregational singing, as if the transformation called for was to become "musical spectators", like the audience at a sports game. Rather, their participation is about entering into the true spirit of the liturgy, and is expressed at different times in the liturgy through singing, attentive listening, and sacred silence.

## *Tensions in* Musicam sacram

*The 1967 Instruction on Music in the Liturgy,* Musicam sacram, *seems to resolve some questions, such as how we should understand actual participation, while at the same time, it seems to promote a somewhat different vision for the implementation of* Sacrosanctum concilium *than you have described. For example, it states, "It is*

[14] Benedict XVI, motu proprio *Summorum pontificum* (July 7, 2007).

*desirable that the assembly of the faithful should participate in the songs of the Proper as much as possible, especially through simple responses and other suitable settings.*"[15] *Taken at face value, it seems to say that since the Gregorian chant settings of the propers are usually too difficult for congregational singing, they should be effectively discarded in favor of simpler settings that could allow for congregational singing. Also, paragraph 34 states that the ordinary of the Mass may be sung to polyphonic settings "as long as the people are not completely excluded from taking part in the singing". However, the vast majority of the treasury of sacred music that* Sacrosanctum concilium *said should be preserved (para. 114) is choral music, not congregational music. It seems that if these words of* Musicam sacram *are followed to the letter, then most of the treasury of sacred music would effectively be thrown out—a reality that most churches witnessed following the Council. And since* Musicam sacram *states that it is preferable for the Sanctus to be sung congregationally (para. 34), is it never appropriate for the choir to sing the entire Sanctus alone, without the congregation singing along? Are there not times when it may be appropriate to have the Schola Cantorum sing all of the propers and ordinary alone, without the congregation singing along except for the responses of the Mass?*

*Musicam sacram* acknowledges that certain portions of the Mass—such as the propers—can be handed over to the choir or Schola while the people participate in other parts that belong to them. However, its caution against completely excluding the people from singing any of the proper and ordinary has led some to question whether a choral Sanctus, for instance, is ever permissible. In his book *A New Song for the Lord*, Cardinal Ratzinger (later Pope Benedict XVI) directly addresses this question. He responds to the argument

[15] *Sacrosanctum concilium*, no. 33.

put forth by liturgist E.J. Lengeling, who argues that the Sanctus must always be sung by the congregation in order to preserve its acclamatory character. Ratzinger writes:

> With all due respect for the eminent liturgist, his opinion shows that even experts can be wide of the mark. First of all, mistrust is always in order when a large part of the living history has to be thrown onto the garbage dump of discarded misunderstandings. This is all the more true for the Christian liturgy, which lives from the continuity and inner unity of the history of religious prayer.[16]

Ratzinger goes on to explain the theological significance of the Sanctus, which invites the congregation to join in the praise of the heavenly choirs. He argues that this expression of praise can occur in a variety of ways, and that the choir can play a representative role for the congregation:

> If the congregation has a choir that can draw it into cosmic praise and into the open expanse of heaven and earth more powerfully than its own stammering, then the representative function of the choir is at this moment particularly appropriate. Through the choir a greater transparency to the praise of the angels and therefore a more profound, interior joining in with their singing are bestowed than a congregation's own acclamation and song would be capable of doing in many places.[17]

Furthermore, Ratzinger suggests that a period of "filled silence" during the choral Sanctus can be beneficial for the congregation's interior participation:

> Does it not do us good, before we set off into the center of the mystery, to encounter a short time of filled silence

[16] Pope Benedict XVI (Joseph Ratzinger), "Sing Artistically for God", in *A New Song for the Lord*, 179.

[17] Ibid., 180.

> in which the choir calms us interiorly, leading each one of us into silent prayer and thus into a union that can occur only on the inside? Must we not relearn this silent, inner co-praying with each other and with the angels and saints, the living and the dead, and with Christ himself?[18]

*It appears then that the writers of* Musicam sacram *may have not fully shared the perspective of Cardinal Ratzinger, and, at times, themselves gave mixed signals about the profound value of silent and prayerful listening as a form of actual participation in the liturgy.*

Yes, I think that despite the best intentions of the Second Vatican Council, there remains a lack of clarity in teaching the true meaning of actual participation, something that is even evident in *Musicam sacram* itself. This is why I think theologians like Cardinal Ratzinger felt compelled to offer their more nuanced perspectives that are rooted in the Church's cultural and liturgical tradition. However, it is worthy to note that these critiques have yet to be adequately integrated into the Church's official liturgical documents. We must remember that the various reforms that the Church carries out through councils and synods can sometimes be expressed imperfectly or even imprudently, and it is our responsibility to interpret them in good faith and with careful reading, always with fidelity to the Church's tradition.

[18] Ibid., 181–82.

5

# CONTEMPLATION, SILENCE, AND SACRED MUSIC

PETER CARTER: *Your Eminence, in the previous chapter, we explored the importance of active participation in the liturgy, emphasizing that silence and listening is an equally valuable form of participation alongside singing. Building upon this foundation, I would like to turn our attention to the relationship between contemplation, silence, and liturgical music, and how they work together in liturgical prayer. Since contemplation is often described by spiritual writers as the highest personal form of prayer, can contemplative prayer be expressed through both sacred silence and sacred music?*

ROBERT CARDINAL SARAH: Silence is not merely an expression of contemplative prayer; it is a necessary condition without which contemplation becomes difficult or even impossible. In my book *God or Nothing*, I described contemplative prayer as follows:

> On the Christian level, contemplation is actually an intimate conversation with God in silence and solitude. It is impossible in the agitation of the world, but even more so in the distractions of interior noise. The tumults that are most difficult to contain are still our own interior storms.
>
> With Christ, contemplation resembles the joy of two lovers who look silently at each other. . . . In love, words are not necessary. The more dense the life of silence, the

more alone the soul is with God. And the more virginal the soul, the more it withdraws from the agitated world."[1]

Sacred music, when it is truly prayer, is born from silence. Even though music is made of both sound and silence, it is created and expressed on a canvas of a prior and fundamental silence, both interior and exterior. Whether we are meditating in silence, actively listening, or engaged with singing, the wonder evoked by the beauty of music can draw us deeper into contemplation and also be an expression of contemplative prayer.

## *Overcoming the Dictatorship of Noise*

*You have previously spoken of a "dictatorship of noise", not music, as the opposite of silence. With this in mind, how should silence be understood in relation to sacred music?*

Everything serious and divine originates in silence. As Romano Guardini says: "The greatest things are accomplished in silence—not in the clamor and display of superficial eventfulness, but in the deep clarity of inner vision; in the almost imperceptible start of decision, in quiet overcoming and hidden sacrifice."[2] As I wrote in *The Power of Silence*, "The silence that we pursue confusedly is found in our own hearts and reveals God to us."[3] It is the foundation, the ground where creation takes root. However, silence is not an end in itself: God speaks in silence, but His voice is what matters; silence is the root, but it is the fruit of what

[1] Robert Cardinal Sarah, *God or Nothing* (Ignatius Press, 2015), 209.

[2] Romano Guardini, *The Lord* (Henry Regnery, 1954), 13.

[3] Robert Cardinal Sarah with Nicolas Diat, *The Power of Silence: Against the Dictatorship of Noise*, trans. Michael J. Miller (Ignatius Press, 2017), 24.

it generates that is important. In this way, music is born of silence, and the beauty of God expressed through the music itself can move us toward the lifting up of our hearts where we praise God with our whole beings. As Saint Augustine writes in one of his Discourses:

> Sing to him "with songs of joy." This is singing well to God, just singing with songs of joy. But how is this done? You must first understand that words cannot express the things that are sung by the heart. . . . Such a cry of joy is a sound signifying that the heart is bringing to birth what it cannot utter in words. Now, who is more worthy of such a cry of jubilation than God himself, whom all words fail to describe? If words will not serve, and yet you must not remain silent, what else can you do but cry out for joy. . . . Sing to him with jubilation.[4]

Joseph Ratzinger eloquently describes this movement of the heart in the context of the liturgy:

> When man comes into contact with God, mere speech is not enough. Areas of his existence are awakened that spontaneously turn into song. Indeed, man's own being is insufficient for what he has to express, and so he invites the whole of creation to become a song with him: "Awake, my soul! Awake, O harp and lyre! I will awake the dawn! I will give thanks to you, O Lord, among the peoples; I will sing praises to you among the nations. For your steadfast love is great to the heavens, your faithfulness to the clouds" (Ps 57:8–10). We find the first mention of singing in the Bible after the crossing of the Red Sea. Israel has now been definitively delivered from slavery. In a desperate situation, it has had an overwhelming experience of God's

[4] Saint Augustine, Discourse on Psalm 32, in *The Liturgy of the Hours* (Catholic Book Publishing, 1990), Office of Readings, Feast of Saint Cecilia.

> saving power. . . . Liturgical singing is established in the midst of this great historical tension.[5]

## *The Liturgy as Contemplative Prayer*

*Could it be said, then, that the Church's sacred liturgy is in fact an exemplar of contemplative prayer, and that her liturgical music is itself an essential component of this?*

The sacred liturgy can and should lead us toward the contemplation of God, but this is not an automatic process, as this contemplation necessitates a full submission of the heart, mind, and soul to God. Music, as a necessary component of solemn liturgical celebrations, draws hearts toward God and urges us to seek Him through its profound beauty. However, this does not mean that our every experience of the liturgy will be one of perfect contemplation or of spiritual consolation. The heart of man "thirsts for God" (Ps 42:2), as I reflected in *God or Nothing*: "The Father made us for Himself, but our heart is anxious, divided by a dull restlessness. In fact, it is simply waiting to rest in God; he alone can satisfy us. This is why, consciously or not, we are constantly in search of the Father."[6] It is tragic when the very meaning of the liturgy loses its Christocentric character. The liturgy can become for us the place of encounter with Christ or an all-too-human routine of sacred rituals; it can be for us a pledge of eternity by inserting us into the ongoing celestial liturgy, or it can become, at least for us, a "exhibition" of human activity. As I outlined in *God or Nothing*:

[5] Ratzinger, *The Spirit of the Liturgy* (Ignatius Press, 2000), 136–37.
[6] Sarah, *God or Nothing*, 211.

> In the commentary on the Gospel of John by Saint Thomas Aquinas, there is a particularly illuminating passage. Jesus turns to Andrew and John, who have asked him: "Rabbi (which means Teacher), where are you staying?" And he answers: "Come and see." Saint Thomas thus gives a mystical sense to words that actually mean that only an encounter and personal experience can enable us to know Christ. This experiential knowledge of God in us is the heart of contemplation. Christ's sacred humanity is always the way by which to arrive at God: to allow him to speak in the silence, before the Blessed Sacrament, looking at a crucifix, in the presence of a sick person who is another Christ, Christ himself. . . .
>
> It would be regrettable if prayer turned into long, vague chatter that led us away from authentic contemplation. Garrulous prayer does not allow the soul to hear God. This is a danger of modern life, in which silence sometimes becomes disturbing. We ceaselessly need to hear the noise of the world: today logorrhea is a sort of imperative, and silence is considered a failure. . . .
>
> Contemplation is a precious moment in the encounter between man and God. The battle continues, but that is the price of the superb victory.[7]

Liturgical prayer is "the action of Christ and the Church", but always in the name of Christ, the only mediator. When Christ is no longer at the center of our prayer, we give glory no longer to Him, but rather to ourselves. And when Christ is no longer at the center of the liturgy—as Pope Benedict observed—He is no longer at the center of our life.

[7] Ibid., 209–10.

## *Preparing the Heart for the Liturgy*

*Most people understand contemplation as belonging only to private prayer, but you are suggesting that it also belongs in the liturgy, as a form of actual participation that can be expressed through both silence and music. What is the relation between private contemplative prayer and liturgical prayer?*

Our Lord Jesus commanded us to pray alone, in front of our Father, behind closed doors:

> And when you pray, you must not be like the hypocrites; for they love to stand and pray in the synagogues and at the street corners, that they may be seen by men. Truly, I say to you, they have their reward. But when you pray, go into your room and shut the door and pray to your Father who is in secret; and your Father who sees in secret will reward you (Mt 6:5–6).

Private prayer, profound and deeply intimate, prepares the soul for public and liturgical prayer. Without true faith and sincerity in our behavior and moral conduct, without charity and true fraternal communion, without this personal and intimate encounter with God, without purity of heart, our participation in public prayer has no value. The book of Amos underscores the futility of public prayer when it is not a genuine expression of the heart:

> I hate, I despise your feasts, and I take no delight in your solemn assemblies. Even though you offer me burnt offerings and cereal offerings, I will not accept them, and the peace offerings of your fatted beasts I will not look upon. Take away from me the noise of your songs; to the melody of your harps I will not listen. But let justice roll down like waters, and righteousness like an ever-flowing stream!" (Amos 5:21–24).

Our experience of Christ in prayer should convict our hearts to reform our lives so that we might give fitting praise to God. We can echo Isaiah's words as our own: "Woe is me! For I am lost; for I am a man of unclean lips, and I dwell in the midst of a people of unclean lips; yet my eyes have seen the King, the LORD of hosts!" (Is 6:5) We are all sinners and need purification to enter God's presence. This purification is vital for our encounter with God in the liturgy, allowing us to sing with humble hearts and perfect praise. God places "a new song" in our mouths as a reflection of this purification. Before the celebration of the liturgy, we should recollect ourselves, asking God to prepare our hearts properly to speak to Him. Our objective is not just to glorify God through the sacred words and music of the liturgy, but also that His glory may be manifested through the holiness of our lives.

Let us recall the writings on prayer of Saint Cyprian, bishop of Carthage (249–258):

> But let those who pray have words and petitions governed by restraint and possessing a quiet modesty. Let us bear in mind that we stand in the sight of God. We must be pleasing in the sight of God both with the habit of body and the measure of voice. For as it is characteristic of the impudent to be noisy with clamors, so on the other hand does it benefit the modest to pray with moderate petitions. . . . And when we are gathered together with the brethren in one place and celebrate divine sacrifices with a priest of God, we ought to be mindful of modesty and discipline, and not toss our prayers about at random with uncouth voices and not cast forth with turbulent loquaciousness our petition, which should be commended to God in modesty, because the hearer is not of the voice but of the heart, and is not to be admonished by shouts, who sees our thoughts, as the Lord proves when He says: 'Why do you think vainly

in your hearts?' And in another place: "And all the churches shall know that I am a searcher of the desires and the heart."[8]

## *Singing as an Act of Love*

*How should we understand Saint Augustine's often-quoted dictum that "to sing well is to pray twice"?*

While Saint Augustine did not write that exact phrase, he did write, "Cantare amantis est"—that is, "Singing is for the one who loves." This profound statement reveals that prayerful singing is ultimately an act of love. It is not our voice that God primarily listens to, but our heart, which expresses itself through music. Good things flow from a heart that is truly in love with God. Therefore, prayer should emanate not just from our lips but from the depths of our being. It can even be silent, for God hears the silent yearnings of our hearts. Private prayer and contemplation is necessary for everyone, and the liturgy, in turn, brings our prayers to the communal dimension proper to the universal Church.

The power of sacred music lies in its ability to bring our hearts into the contemplation of God. As Pope Benedict stated: "Music is capable of opening minds and hearts to the dimension of the spirit and leads people to lift their gaze to the Most High, to open themselves to the absolute Good and Beauty whose ultimate source is in God."[9] While it is a good thing to have our voices sing in a beautiful and aesthetically pleasing way, true beauty in prayer always

[8] Saint Cyprian, "The Lord's Prayer", in *The Fathers of the Church*, vol. 36, *Treatises of Saint Cyprian*, trans. and ed. Roy J. Deferrari (Fathers of the Church, 1958), 129–30.

[9] Benedict XVI, Address on the Occasion of the Fifth Anniversary of His Pontificate (Paul VI Audience Hall, April 29, 2010).

stems from the heart. Some may not have a naturally beautiful singing voice, yet they can still sing from their heart with faith, love, sincerity, and devotion. As Pope Benedict also writes, "Prayer is a gift of the Holy Spirit, both prayer in general and that particular kind of prayer which is the gift of singing and playing before God. The Holy Spirit is love. He enkindles love in us and thus moves us to sing."[10]

We need only recall the experience of Saint Augustine: "How copiously I wept at your hymns and canticles, how intensely was I moved by the lovely harmonies of your singing Church! Those voices flooded my ears, and the truth was distilled into my heart until it overflowed in loving devotion; my tears ran down, and I was the better for them."[11] Similarly, Paul Claudel, a French poet, playwright, and diplomat, who was initially a nonbeliever, recounts his powerful conversion experience at the Christmas Mass at Notre-Dame Cathedral in Paris, upon hearing the singing of the Magnificat:

> In a single instant my heart was touched, and I believed. I believed with such an intensity of acceptance, with such an uplifting of my whole being, with such a power of conviction, with such certitude, leaving no room for any sort of doubt, that since then all the books, all the arguments, all the hazards of an active life have not succeeded in shaking my faith nor, to tell the truth, in touching it.[12]

[10] Ratzinger, *The Spirit of the Liturgy*, 149.

[11] Saint Augustine, *Confessions*, trans. Maria Boulding, O.S.B. (New City Press, 1997), bk. 9, no. 14.

[12] Paul Claudel, *Contacts et circonstances*, 12, quoted in Paul Claudel, *I Believe in God: A Meditation on the Apostles' Creed*, trans. Helen Weaver (Holt, Reinhart and Winston, 1963), 3.

*What advice would you give to the lay faithful who feel that they do not have the ability or the interest to sing?*

Modern man readily has music at his disposal, but he is often not fully formed and matured into becoming a musical being. To sing requires a certain selflessness, a giving of one's voice that may feel uncomfortable or unsettling, especially if one has not learned to do it well and is self-conscious about what others might think. It is true that some individuals are more contemplative and silent by nature, and we must respect this. However, we must also help and encourage them to pray and sing with the faithful in the liturgy at the appropriate times. It is important to educate the faithful to understand that they are part of a whole, members of the Body of Christ. As such, they are generally expected to participate in communal actions, such as singing, to the extent that they are able. Just as blood nourishes every part of the body, each member of the Church has a role to play in the liturgy. The Church is a living body, and we are all called to pray as a united body, a body that at times sings the praises of God, and a body that at times silently beholds Him. However, if someone honestly does not feel capable of singing with his voice, he can still truly "sing with the heart". Every time I have visited Assisi, I have been struck by the text in the choir of the Church of San Damiano: "Non vox sed votum; non clamor sed amor, non cordula sed cor psallit in aure Dei. Vox concordet menti, mens autem concordet cum Deo"—that is, "Not the voice, but the desire. Not the noise, but the love. Not the strings, but the heart sings in the ear of God. The voice accords with the mind and the mind with God." This sentiment is echoed in various passages of Scripture, as Saint Cyprian writes:

> Hannah in the first book of Kings, who was a type of the Church, maintains and observes, in that she prayed to God not with clamorous petition, but silently and modestly, within the very recesses of her heart. She spoke with hidden prayer, but with manifest faith. She spoke not with her voice, but with her heart, because she knew that thus God hears; and she effectually obtained what she sought, because she asked it with belief. . . .We read also in the Psalms, "*Speak in your hearts, and in your beds, and be pierced.*" The Holy Spirit, moreover, suggests these same things by Jeremiah, and teaches, saying, "*But in the heart ought God to be adored by you.*"[13]

We also see a beautiful example of humble, silent prayer in the Gospel account of the tax collector and the Pharisee (Lk 18:9–14). The tax collector did not pray ostentatiously but beat his breast and confessed his sins, imploring God's mercy. It was he, not the self-righteous Pharisee, who went home justified. Like him, we must learn to pray with the heart, humbly and in silence. Saint Bernardine of Siena had these words inscribed in the sanctuary at Fonte Colombo, where his friars prayed the liturgy of the hours: "*Si cor non orat, in vanum lingua laborat.*"—If the heart does not pray, the tongue labors in vain. It is crucial that we do not insert ourselves into our prayer, praying only according to our own unique preferences and customs, "for we do not know how to pray as we ought" (Rom 8:26). Rather, we must approach God with modesty, humility, and sincerity, echoing the disciples' request to Jesus: "Lord, teach us to pray" (Lk 11:1).

[13] Saint Cyprian, *Treatise 4: On the Lord's Prayer*, no. 5, in *Ante-Nicene Fathers*, vol. 5, trans. Robert Ernest Wallis, ed. Alexander Roberts, James Donaldson, and A. Cleveland Coxe (Christian Literature Publishing Co., 1886), revised and edited for New Advent by Kevin Knight, accessed July 2, 2025, https://www.newadvent.org/fathers/050704.htm.

## *Diversity in Unity Is "Polyphony"*

ROBERT CARDINAL SARAH: To conclude this discussion on music and contemplation, I would like to share some beautiful passages from Giuseppe Liberto, an Italian priest and composer who has also served as the director of the Sistine Chapel Choir. At a conference on sacred music in Assisi, he beautifully described the relationship between music, silence, and the liturgy: "I often define music as a staff of silence punctuated by vibrations of sound and light. The mystical staff of silence in liturgical celebration is punctuated by two vibrations of sound and light: the Word of God that comes to us in the Word and the Eucharist within the Ecclesial Body, and our perpetual praise that rises to God like the scent of incense."[14] Liberto goes on to emphasize the transformative power of silence and its ability to illuminate the Word of God, allowing it to become life-giving and to take root in the hearts of the faithful: "Silence is the light that illuminates the Word so that it becomes life-giving, and light causes the Word to sprout in the heart of man so that it becomes a song of praise, supplication, and thanksgiving." He also highlights the importance of unity in diversity within the liturgical celebration, drawing from Saint Paul:

> In this way, the assembly that celebrates by singing realizes, in the variety of different voices, the harmony of the one *agape* and manifests the unity of being together in multiplicity. The 'musical,' in fact, by its nature, is both polyphony and unison. In liturgical celebration, the polyphony of the

[14] Giuseppe Liberto, "L'arte musicale, privilegiato ponte tra il trascendente e il cuore dell'uomo", paper presented at the conference "La missione della musica sacra secondo Papa Francesco", hosted by the Associazione Italiana Santa Cecilia, Assisi, Italy, March 9–12, 2020.

> choir is the expression of diversity in unity. 'Although there are many of us, we are one body,' says St. Paul (1 Corinthians 12:17). The unison of the assembly is the expression of unity in plurality, and again St. Paul writes: 'There is one body and one Spirit, just as you were called to one hope when you were called; one Lord, one faith, one baptism; one God and Father of all, who is over all and through all and in all' (Eph 4:4–6).

Liberto emphasizes that every aspect of the liturgy should be oriented toward building up the one Body of Christ, with Christ as the source, model, and goal of all liturgical art:

> In the celebration of the *agape*, the Logos-Melos aims at the building of universal and cosmic human communion. Every plurality is therefore oriented towards the building of the one Body of Christ: one Body, one Spirit. . . . Christ is the end, the purpose, the subject, and the material of true liturgical art; He, the Word of God made flesh of our human nature, who died for us men and for our salvation; He, the Light of the nations, the Splendor of the Father's Glory, risen, celebrated, and sung by His Church and in His Church; He, the Joy and Hope who came to transform man, history, and the cosmos.

Liberto also warns of the danger of distorting the praise of God into a blasphemous song if our lives lack truth, love, and authenticity: "The gesture of singing belongs to those who are capable of true love. Only in this way can Christ's prayerful desire be realized: 'That they may all be one' (Jn 17:21). Only in this way are we capable of singing, with one heart and one soul, the hymn of *agape*: 'Where true charity is, God is there. Together we have been gathered into one by Christ's love.'"[15]

[15] Ibid.

Without truth in our lives, our songs and religious practices are reduced to mere community gatherings in which we entertain ourselves, while God turns His gaze away from us. True worship that is pleasing to God is an offering of ourselves with Him as a living sacrifice (see Rom 12:1), the same sacrifice that Christ commanded us to offer in remembrance of Him at the Last Supper:

> And he took a chalice, and when he had given thanks he said, "Take this, and divide it among yourselves; for I tell you that from now on I shall not drink of the fruit of the vine until the kingdom of God comes." And he took bread, and when he had given thanks he broke it and gave it to them, saying, "This is my body, which is given for you. Do this in remembrance of me" (Lk 22:17–19).

Whenever we lose sight of our personal relationship with God, it is a spiritual crisis that is manifested through the superficiality in our prayers and the hypocrisy in our lives. Whether we pray privately in our homes or publicly in the liturgy, we must cultivate our personal and intimate relationship with Christ, the God who became man so that we might be fully united with Him! Christ always seeks us first, and we treasure and cultivate this relationship with Christ through our contemplation and worship of Him.

# Part III

# The Crisis of Liturgical Culture

6

# THE PRESERVATION OF LATIN AND GREGORIAN CHANT

PETER CARTER: *Among the liturgical reforms described in the Second Vatican Council's Constitution on the Sacred Liturgy, Sacrosanctum concilium, was the allowance of a broader use of the vernacular in the liturgy—a significant change from the Church's liturgical praxis for centuries. What was the purpose of allowing vernacular languages to be introduced into the liturgy? And what were the Council's intentions regarding the continued use of Latin?*

ROBERT CARDINAL SARAH: The Second Vatican Council clearly stated that "the use of the Latin language is to be preserved in the Latin Rites."[1] Nevertheless, in its wisdom, the Council recognized that a limited allowance of vernacular languages could be of great benefit to the faithful in their understanding of and participation in the Church's liturgical life: "But since the use of the mother tongue, whether in the Mass, the administration of the sacraments, or other parts of the liturgy, frequently may be of great advantage to the people, the limits of its employment may be extended. This will apply in the first place to the readings and directives, and to some of the prayers and chants."[2] The Council's intention was twofold: On one hand, it wanted to make the liturgy

[1] Vatican Council II, Constitution on the Sacred Liturgy *Sacrosanctum concilium* (December 4, 1963), no. 36.

[2] Ibid.

more accessible to modern man, thereby helping the faithful more readily understand and participate in the Church's worship. On the other hand, it also recognized Latin's irreplaceable value in both unifying the universal Church and preserving its ancient liturgical traditions. The Council envisioned a balanced use of Latin and vernacular languages, with the sacred language of Latin remaining an integral part of the liturgy, and the vernacular to enable the faithful to understand more easily the sacred Scriptures in the liturgical celebrations.

When Pope Paul VI published the Novus Ordo Missae in 1969, allowing for the entire Mass to be celebrated in the vernacular, he intended for it to foster greater participation in the liturgy, though what consequently followed in many places—perhaps most—was that Latin all but disappeared from the Church's liturgical life, despite the Council's call for its preservation. Recognizing this unfortunate reality and the urgent need to uphold the Council's call for the preservation of Latin and Gregorian chant, the Sacred Congregation for Divine Worship issued the letter *Voluntati obsequens* in 1974 with an accompanying booklet called *Jubilate Deo*, which outlined a minimum repertoire of Latin Gregorian chants to be sung in cathedrals and parishes throughout the world.

*This letter was issued to preserve the use of Latin Gregorian chants in the Novus Ordo Missae?*

Yes. The effective disappearance of Gregorian chant from liturgical celebrations necessitated a clarification and reassurance that the faithful can and should still participate in the liturgy using the Church's universal language, and that the Church's musical tradition, which was almost entirely in Latin, was still relevant and needed to be preserved. *Voluntati obsequens* was a heartfelt plea to the Church to implement the desires of Paul VI "that all the faithful should know at least some Latin Gregorian chants, such as, for example, the '*Gloria*', the '*Credo*', the '*Sanctus*', and the '*Agnus Dei*'",[3] which was itself an echo of the words of the Second Vatican Council that "steps should be taken so that the faithful may also be able to say or sing together in Latin those parts of the Ordinary of the Mass which pertain to them."[4] The accompanying booklet of chants, titled *Jubilate Deo*, was meant as an aid to churches throughout the world to make this a reality.

These documents served two essential purposes. First, they reminded the Church that the Council's vision for liturgical participation was broader than just the utilization of vernacular and, in fact, included continuing use of the venerable and ancient music of Gregorian chant. Second, they provided a practical means for maintaining a unity in the Church's liturgical celebrations across the universal Church. The simple chants included in *Jubilate Deo* offered a shared musical language that was truly sacred and liturgical and rooted in the Church's tradition. When one listens to and sings these melodies, one is drawn into the very act of worship. Over time, the Latin language becomes familiar and comforting, and the liturgy becomes understood as a complete act of worship rooted in the Church's immutable

[3] Sacred Congregation for Divine Worship, Letter to the Bishops on the Minimum Repertoire of Plain Chant *Voluntati obsequens* (April 14, 1974), https://adoremus.org/2007/12/voluntati-obsequens/. Paul VI, General Audience (August 22, 1973); Paul VI, Address to the Consociatio Internationalis Musicae Sacrae (October 12, 1973); Letter of Cardinal Jean Villot to the National Assembly of the Italian Association of Saint Cecilia, September 30, 1973.

[4] *Sacrosanctum concilium*, no. 54.

tradition, not limited to the changeable vernacular translations in the latest edition of the Missal.

*This brings us back to the third criterion for sacred music outlined in* Tra le sollecitudini*—universality. As you mentioned, Latin helps to maintain unity in the Church as a universal language. However, some may counter that since Latin is not a spoken language, it can in fact hinder the actual participation in the liturgy sought by* Sacrosanctum concilium.

Actual participation in the liturgy is not a question of intellectual comprehension; it is a question of faith. Sadly, I think it is very common for people to attend liturgies where they can comprehend every word, but inwardly their faith is dead, making it impossible for them truly to participate. The Latin language should not be seen as a barrier to participation, even if people understand very little of it. Rather, because it is the sacred language of the Latin Church, it is a door for people to experience the sacredness of the liturgy, which can have a profound effect on their faith, and consequently, their participation in the sacred mysteries.

There is a strong similarity in this regard with the religion of Islam. Muslims speak many different languages in their daily lives, but when they come to pray, they are united in their use of Arabic, their shared movements and postures, and their common orientation toward Mecca. In a similar way, the liturgy of the Catholic Church unites all the Christian faithful in the worship of the one true God, regardless of their distinct cultural identities.

## *Latin as a Sacred Language*

*How important is it for the faithful to grasp every word of the liturgy? If I understand correctly, from your own childhood and growth in the faith, the sacredness you experienced in the Mass enabled you to understand its importance even before possessing a thorough knowledge of Latin or the liturgy.*

When I was a child, I couldn't understand everything in the Latin Mass. But through learning to sing in the Mass—the Gloria, the Credo, etc.—I learned how to express my love for God through the words and music of the liturgy. Praying is not just a question of understanding; it is a question of listening to God and kneeling before Him in adoration and love. What is most important in prayer is that my heart is talking to God. This is much simpler and profound than merely comprehending every single word.

When I say in the Holy Mass, "This is My Body" and "this is My Blood", I understand what I am saying; I know the words. But if I don't believe, it is nothing! It is the Holy Spirit who changes the bread into the Body of Christ and the wine into the Blood of Christ, not something that I can do of my own capacity. I have an intellectual understanding of what is happening, but only faith makes it true and genuine! The disciples asked our Lord, "Increase our faith" (Lk 17:5). We too must ask our Lord to increase our faith—even we priests—to believe truly that what we are doing is really what we are saying. Faith is a gift from God, and God wants us to grow in faith through our participation in the liturgy. If we open ourselves to God and to His work in us, then He will increase our faith little by little.

This approach toward praying the liturgy strikes me as similar to the way we teach children the alphabet through the alphabet song. They certainly do not understand the letters at first, but over time they come to learn what they mean through repetition and ongoing education. Is the same true of the *Jubilate Deo* chants, since they are meant to be accessible to everyone?

It is not necessary to have a detailed knowledge of every

component of liturgical prayer in order for it to be sincere and from the heart. As Saint John Damascene says, prayer is simply raising the heart and mind to God and requesting good things from God.[5] Though we may not grasp every word, the Latin language draws us together in the tradition of the Church to participate in the sacred mysteries. Preaching, listening to the Word of God, and religious devotions—these are good in our own vernacular languages. But we must have humility! God willed that the Church should have her own sacred language and her own tradition of sacred music through which to praise God. We must be humble, like children, if we are to learn the language and music of the Church, the language and music of God! If we use only our own language and our own music, we can become focused exclusively on ourselves and close ourselves off from the rest of the Church—we may even close ourselves off from God! When we chant the Credo in Latin, we are opening ourselves to the whole Church—we are united with Chinese Christians, with Arabic Christians, etc. We are not alone. God wants the Church to be a family! God showed this in the Old Testament with His covenant with Abraham and in the New Testament with the twelve Apostles when He founded the Church. A family must have a shared language, a shared culture, shared customs. If we lose Latin, we lose this shared bond with the Church throughout the world; we lose catholicity.

*I have heard some people say that using Latin in their parishes is "not the way we do things here". And I have heard some bishops and priests express the fear of having "too much Latin" in the liturgy, as some of the faithful may react negatively toward it. Is this fear of Latin misplaced? Is it ever justified?*

[5] Saint John of Damascus, *On the Orthodox Faith*, trans. Norman Russell (St. Vladmir's Seminary Press, 2022), bk. 3, chap. 24.

I think that what lies behind this combative attitude toward Latin is generations of poor formation rooted in an ideology that the Church's tradition must be discarded for something entirely new. The Church allows the use of the vernacular in the liturgy, but the Council is clear that Latin is to be retained as the language of the Roman Church, and that all the faithful should know the Latin chant settings of the ordinary of the Mass—the Gloria, Credo, Sanctus, and Agnus Dei—as well as the Kyrie, which is in Greek. And even when the vernacular is used in the liturgy, it must always be sufficiently sacred so that it will bring us closer to God, not to the everyday things of the world. If we truly want to implement the Council's liturgical vision for the Church, then we cannot regard Latin as antithetical to the actual participation of the faithful in the liturgy. I want to be clear: Rejecting the Church's tradition, including the Latin language and the singing of Gregorian chant, is indeed a rejection of the Second Vatican Council.

*I have found that especially when older Catholics experience a liturgy that is different from what they are familiar with, even a beautiful liturgy that perfectly follows the rubrics, they can feel repulsed by it. I have seen this sometimes happen at parishes where the parishioners are used to experiencing a liturgy solely in the vernacular and the pastor reintroduces Latin or Gregorian chant to parts of the liturgy. The Latin can feel foreign to them, and they can even feel as if they are being told that the way they are used to praying is either wrong or not good enough. How should the faithful be taught to appreciate and participate in an unfamiliar expression of liturgical prayer?*

It is clear that the Church asks that the faithful should be instructed in the Latin words and chants of the Mass, especially those found in the *Jubilate Deo* booklet. How this instruction is done at a parish is something the pastor must decide with prudence and discretion, but also with fortitude.

He should not be discouraged at the first sign of discontent but must lead his flock with patience and diligence. Van Gogh beautifully expressed that "Those who love much, do much and accomplish much, and whatever is done with love is done well."[6] The same is true for a pastor who loves his flock.

Great patience and pastoral care must be given to those who may possess a contempt for Latin or for any part of the Church's tradition. In these extreme cases, we should always respond with charity and pray for them through the words of Christ: "Father, forgive them; for they know not what they do" (Lk 23:34). Nevertheless, we should not be afraid of the tradition of the Church as if it were somehow damaging or no longer beneficial to the Church today. To some, it may be a distasteful medicine. But a good parent gives his child his medicine even if he may not want it, though always with tenderness, patience, and love.

*I have noticed that at least in English there is a line drawn in the sand with the vernacularization of the liturgy: Even those who advocate against the inclusion of Latin and the Greek "Kyrie eleison" in the liturgy never argue that we should not use the sacred Hebrew words of "Amen" and "Alleluia".*

The faithful may not always be able to explain the precise meaning of certain sacred words or gestures, but they can intuitively understand what they mean from their context in the sacred liturgy. How much would be lost if we discarded those sacred words of God's chosen people! Indeed, God will punish us if we desecrate what has been consecrated. We must not destroy what is sacred! When priests impose their ideology on the people of God, it is a scandal. We need

[6] Letter of Vincent van Gogh to Theo van Gogh, April 3, 1878, in Vincent van Gogh, *The Letters of Vincent van Gogh*, ed. Ronald de Leeuw, trans. Arnold Pomerans (Penguin Books, 1997), 53.

good priests! We need holy priests. We need men of God to lead the people of God to the Promised Land, the heavenly liturgy. And we must educate the faithful and especially the future generations of priests and bishops so that they will come to know and love the Church's tradition and liturgy when it is properly and beautifully celebrated. We must not approach the liturgy with any ideology. Instead, we must have great humility when we pray, "for we do not know how to pray as we ought" (Rom 8:26).

*It seems that entirely replacing Latin with the vernacular in the liturgy has not resulted in a widespread rediscovery of the sacredness of the liturgy or a wave of religious renewal.*

The doctrines of the Church have never changed and will never change, but there has been much radical change in the Church's post-conciliar liturgical praxis. The Council intended an openness to the vernacular as a means of evangelization and sanctification, but what we see today is a far more extensive use of the vernacular than what the Council intended. Tragically, the liturgy in most places has become humanized, more like man. This is a real crisis in the Church today, and it is why Pope Benedict's vision for the renewal of the liturgy is the way forward to sanctifying the Church today.

*I think that there is a common misunderstanding today, perhaps because the liturgy is celebrated so often entirely in the vernacular, that the faithful must follow along with every word and know what is happening at every moment.*

When the liturgy becomes merely a text to recite or a program to follow, it is very easy to forget that the liturgy is a mystical prayer that we must pray from the depths of our hearts. The heart has to be listening to God's voice, which presents itself to us in a myriad of ways in the sacred liturgy. When we encounter a sacred language, as Latin is for Catholics or Arabic is for Muslims, it teaches us that we are entering into something sacred. Sadly, the complete vernacularization of the liturgy has contributed to the loss of the sense of sacredness the Church experiences today.

*I have noticed that if we lose a sense of the sacredness of the liturgy, then we can tend to approach the Scriptures merely as tools for our own edification in the same manner that we might benefit from the wise words of a philosopher.*

The Scriptures themselves are a revelation of God's presence in the world. That is why John's Gospel recounts that Christ is the Word incarnate. The liturgy invites us into a contemplation of Christ through His presence in the Scriptures, and through the mystery of Christ's sacrifice on the cross, made truly present at every Eucharistic celebration. The Scriptures are not meant merely to be read and studied, but to be prayed, to be contemplated, meditated upon, and interiorized! The psalms of David remain the hymns of the Church today, just as they were sung in the Temple worship of the Old Testament. The Church reveals to us the treasures of the Scriptures throughout the liturgical year, through which we meditate on the life of Christ and through which we pray to the Father through Him. Through our encounter with Christ in the Scriptures, we too can touch our Lord's hem and receive His grace and healing.

## *Participation Is Accessible for All*

*If participation in liturgical prayer is simply the lifting of our hearts and minds to God through the liturgy, then it also seems universally accessible because it does not discriminate in favor of only literate youth and adults, but includes people of all ages and with any form of physical or cognitive disability. Is that a correct understanding?*

Yes! Christ said, "Let the children come to me, and do not hinder them; for to such belongs the kingdom of heaven" (Mt 19:14). The experience of the Church's liturgy is an encounter with beauty, both created and uncreated, forming the imagination, the mind, and the heart. Whether people realize it or not, they are encountering Jesus Christ. Even if they are unable to speak, babies and those with disabilities can perceive the goodness and beauty of the liturgy, which lifts their hearts to goodness and ultimately to God, who is the source of all goodness. Music, in particular, has a special and mysterious power over the heart, which is why it is often referred to as a universal language that unites all peoples regardless of our level of understanding of the meaning of the words.

*I remember directing the music for Mass several years ago where the choir was singing one of the beautiful gradual chants with a drone (a sustained note) added to ornament it. After the Mass, a little boy about four or five years old came up to me to tell me the music before the Gospel "sounded like heaven". I could tell that he knew exactly what the music was about even though he could not tell me exactly what was sung. His heart was formed by his experience of beauty.*

*Another time, I was visiting my sister and holding my two-year-old niece during Mass. At the Gospel acclamation, the cantor sang a beautiful and simple setting of the Alleluia, and when the congregation repeated it, my musical niece instinctively joined in singing it too, even though she could barely talk. It was a profound realization to me at the time that she was naturally and truly participating in the liturgy according to her capacity.*

If the Church demanded a complete intellectual understanding prior to liturgical participation, then most everyone would be excluded. But this is not the way of Christ, who commanded His Apostles to baptize all nations, all peoples (see Mt 28:19). We should always seek to grow in our understanding of the sacred mysteries according to our capacity, but we must acknowledge that they are mysteries that we can never fully comprehend on this earth. Only in heaven, when we behold God face-to-face, will we be able to understand fully what we "see in a mirror, dimly", as Saint Paul describes the experience (1 Cor 13:12).

As Christian disciples, we must love the Lord first and foremost. And since we become like that which we love, by loving the Lord, we become like Him more and more. And by loving the Son, we become children of God. In relation to the liturgy, we should be "like children", humbly standing before the throne of God, free from all distractions, worldly pursuits, and self-seeking. The liturgy then provides us with a spiritual formation that directs our hearts to God. It is the place where the priest acts as the visible figure of Christ, the alter Christus, indeed *Ipse Christus*: Christ Himself, offering the sacrifice of the cross to the Father. And we must all unite our hearts with His and offer the first fruits of creation for the praise of His glory.

# 7

# AUTHENTIC LITURGICAL INCULTURATION

PETER CARTER: *Your Eminence, those who have read* God or Nothing *will know that your family and village of Ourous in Guinea were first-generation Christians, baptized by French priests of the Holy Ghost Fathers, now known as the Spiritans. What were your earliest experiences with music growing up in your village of Ourous, before you left for the minor seminary?*

ROBERT CARDINAL SARAH: Growing up, I was immersed in a variety of musical traditions. In the village, everyone participated in the singing, not just during religious ceremonies but also during the various festivals that marked the passing of seasons and the milestones of life. From the joyous songs that accompanied the harvest season to the sacred hymns sung during church services, music was an integral part of our community's identity and expression.

*Was the music used in the village's liturgies and the music sung and performed during village festivals completely different, or was there some overlap?*

There was a clear distinction between the music used in the church and that which was part of the village celebrations. The French missionaries who brought the faith to my village taught us the sacred music they knew, primarily Gregorian chant and French hymns. In the church, the use of African drums and traditional African instruments was strictly prohibited, and the organ was the only instrument permitted to be used. The music for the village festivals was rooted in our African heritage, featuring traditional instruments such as the kora, a West African stringed instrument, and drums.

## *Liturgical Unity amid Diversity*

*Your Eminence, as we've discussed in the previous chapter, amid the post-conciliar liturgical reforms that allowed the liturgy to be completely celebrated in vernacular languages, the Church issued the* Jubilate Deo *collections of Gregorian chants to preserve the Latin musical tradition and to maintain unity within the Latin Rite celebrated across the world. However, with the publication of the Novus Ordo Missae in 1969 and the allowance for a complete vernacularization of the liturgy, liturgical celebrations across the world began to include many more distinctive cultural elements, including in the realm of sacred music. While our focus is primarily on sacred music, I would like to begin with a broader question about the balance between unity and diversity. As you said before, the unity in the Roman Rite is expressed liturgically through the Latin language, and in terms of sacred music, especially through Gregorian chant. However, on the other hand, diversity seems to be expressed in almost the exact opposite way: with vernacular liturgical languages and local forms and expressions of sacred music. How does the Church reconcile these two realities?*

The Church is truly universal, embracing people from every nation, race, and language. The inculturation of local or regional elements can bring a diversity of riches to the Church, though not all forms of inculturation are compatible with the reverence demanded by the liturgy. An African Mass may indeed look and sound quite different from one celebrated in Asia, each reflecting the unique cultural expressions of faith in the region. This diversity can truly be a gift, reflecting the beauty of God's creation.

However, in the wake of the Second Vatican Council's reforms, which encouraged greater use of the vernacular in the liturgy, we have witnessed an unsettling rise of adapting the Mass to the secular culture, overshadowing the sacredness and reverence demanded by the Eucharistic celebration. While it is right and fitting to incorporate dignified elements of local culture into the liturgy, this must be done with great care and discernment. The essential elements of the liturgy—the prayers, the readings, the Eucharistic sacrifice, etc.—must remain intact. The cultural adaptations that the Church allows should serve to illuminate the universal truths of the faith, not obscure them.

This is where Gregorian chant and the Latin language can play a vital role. These ancient forms of prayer possess a universal quality that transcends time and place. They belong to the patrimony of the entire Church. When we sing the Gregorian chants of the Mass or hear the prayers proclaimed in Latin, we are reminded that we are part of a Church much larger than our local community—it is the same Church that Christ founded two thousand years ago when He appointed Saint Peter as His vicar on earth, and who then became the first bishop of Rome. Of course, this does not mean that there is no place for other languages or musical styles in the liturgy. In principle, the Church is always open to incorporating the riches of various cultures into her worship. But it is imperative that any cultural adaptations be truly in harmony with the spirit of the liturgy and always subordinate to the unifying power of our common faith, as expressed in the ancient prayers and chants of the Mass.

I remember visiting Sri Lanka, and one day I entered a Buddhist temple. I was amazed by the faith and fervor of the crowd of Buddhists—people who live out the teaching of Gautama Buddha that suffering is inherent in life and that one can be liberated from it by mental and moral self-purification—praying in Sanskrit, an ancient language akin to Latin, yet completely foreign to me with its vertically flowing script. And I recall attending a liturgy led by Cardinal Ranjith, where the faithful were praying in Sinhalese or Tamil. Though I could not understand the words, I recognized the melody of the Credo being sung, which was similar to the Latin chant. If music is truly liturgical like this, it can transcend the boundaries of culture and continent, serving as a link that connects us with the same faith of the early Church.

While the Church has historically permitted some variability in its liturgical celebrations, unity in the observance of holy days reinforces our shared Christian faith throughout the world. This is why a unified celebration of Easter among all Christian churches is a matter of such great importance. The Church does not want a diversity of Easter celebrations; she wants unity on this most holy of days. We must also recognize that diversity can become perilous when it touches upon the essential doctrines of our faith. If someone were to profess that hell is empty or express doubt about the reality of sin, it would indicate a fundamental divergence in belief. True unity requires that we share the same faith and the same creed.

Translations of sacred texts into various languages can, over time, result in subtle shifts in meaning and understanding. We see this today in the various translations of the Lord's Prayer. The Latin, however, steadies the boat amid the changing tides of the age. Translations may change but the truth does not!

## *Understanding Inculturation*

*The term "inculturation" is often used in different ways, sometimes referring to the Church's missionary efforts of integrating the Christian faith into various cultures, and conversely, the process of integrating aspects of cultures into the Church's liturgical or religious practice. The use of the vernacular in the liturgy, the incorporation of local art and architecture in church buildings, and the adaptation of local styles of music into religious celebrations are often pointed to as positive examples of liturgical inculturation. However, you mentioned that there have also been efforts to adapt the Mass to the culture in ways that obscure the nature and purpose of the sacred liturgy. If inculturation is essential to the Church's mission, allowing the faith to take root in the cultures of all nations, how should inculturation be properly understood? And how can we navigate the tension between the universal and local expressions of the Christian faith, particularly when it comes to the sacred liturgy?*

In beginning to answer this question, I will refer to the Second Vatican Council's Pastoral Constitution on the Church in the Modern World, *Gaudium et spes*, which provides valuable insight on the relationship between culture and faith:

> Man comes to a true and full humanity only through culture, that is through the cultivation of the goods and values of nature. Wherever human life is involved, therefore, nature and culture are quite intimately connected one with the other.
>
> The word "culture" in its general sense indicates everything whereby man develops and perfects his many bodily and spiritual qualities; he strives by his knowledge and his labor, to bring the world itself under his control. He renders social life more human both in the family and the civic community, through improvement of customs and institutions. Throughout the course of time he expresses, communicates and conserves in his works, great spiritual

> experiences and desires, that they might be of advantage to the progress of many, even of the whole human family.[1]

This intimate connection between man and culture means that it would be impossible to speak of human worship of the living God divorced from cultural expression.

*Gaudium et spes* continues:

> Thence it follows that human culture has necessarily a historical and social aspect and the word "culture" also often assumes a sociological and ethnological sense. According to this sense we speak of a plurality of cultures. Different styles of life and multiple scales of values arise from the diverse manner of using things, of laboring, of expressing oneself, of practicing religion, of forming customs, of establishing laws and juridic institutions, of cultivating the sciences, the arts and beauty. Thus the customs handed down to it form the patrimony proper to each human community. It is also in this way that there is formed the definite, historical milieu which enfolds the man of every nation and age and from which he draws the values which permit him to promote civilization.[2]

Liturgical inculturation, then, can be understood as the integration of the noble elements of human culture into the act of divine worship. However, the integration of distinct cultural aspects into the liturgy and the life of the Church is not done to fulfill a mandate of cultural inclusion that exists prior to the Church's work of salvation. In the Church's celebration of the divine liturgy, inculturation must be integrated after the fact, not before, since by its very origin, the divine precedes the human. God always loves us first. Christ instituted the sacraments and the liturgy, and through the liturgy He visits us and awaits our response. Through

[1] Vatican II, Pastoral Constitution on the Church in the Modern World *Gaudium et spes* (December 7, 1965), no. 53.

[2] Ibid.

the liturgy, God comes to us in His Truth, Goodness, and Beauty, and our role is to welcome Him.

*Does the Church provide specific principles for discerning between proper and improper inculturation?*

As Pope Saint John Paul II affirmed, "Properly applied, inculturation must be guided by two principles: 'compatibility with the gospel and communion with the universal Church.'"[3] Inculturation can never be an excuse for religious syncretism or doctrinal relativism; it must always serve the unity of faith and the integrity of the Christian faith. As I explained in *The Power of Silence*, inculturation is a much more spiritual and transformational process than simply covering Christianity or the liturgy with a layer of African or Asian paint:

> Inculturation is truly a silent kenosis, a kind of destitution, an obedient, humble submission to the will of the Father and to the Holy Christian mysteries that we celebrate through Jesus Christ, with him and in him.
>
> Indeed, just as through the Incarnation the Word of God became just like men, except for sin (cf. Heb 4:15), so too the Gospel takes up all human and cultural values, but refuses to take shape in the structures of sin. This means that the more abundant individual and collective sin is in a human or an ecclesial community, the less room there is in it for inculturation. Conversely, the more a Christian community shines with sanctity and radiates Gospel values, the more opportunities it has to inculturate the Christian message successfully. The inculturation of the faith is therefore a challenge to holiness. It allows us to determine the degree

[3] John Paul II, encyclical letter *Redemptoris missio* (On the Permanent Validity of the Church's Missionary Mandate) (December 12, 1990), no. 54, quoting John Paul II, apostolic exhortation *Familiaris consortio* (On the Role of the Christian Family in the Modern World) (November 22, 1981), no. 10.

> of sanctity and the level of the penetration of the Gospel and of faith in Jesus Christ in a Christian community. Inculturation is therefore not a type of religious folklore.[4]

That is why Saint Irenaeus says: "Deus homo factus est, ut homo fieret Deus":[5] God became man so that man might become God. Inculturation must divinize man; let God enter into his culture and into his intimate life to configure him, identify him with Jesus Christ, and sanctify him, eliminating the impurities, the scum, and the sins that pollute culture and the human being.

To reiterate what I wrote then, inculturation does not mean a wholesale adoption of every cultural element, regardless of its compatibility with the Christian faith, as this would indeed lead to relativism. There are certain nonnegotiable elements of Christian worship—certain aspects of the sacred tradition that have been passed down to us from the Apostles that cannot be altered without doing violence to the liturgy and to the Christian faith itself. Even as we seek to express the faith in diverse cultural contexts, the Church's essential unity must always be preserved, especially evident in her celebration of the same seven sacraments instituted by Christ. It is crucial to remember that our participation in the liturgy is not simply a human act of worship, but first and foremost our participation in the act of divine worship offered by Jesus Christ to the Father.

The organization of the liturgical action should always preserve the nature of the liturgy itself through discernment. The mediating Christ, the Christ of the liturgy, is the one who comes. In the liturgy, Christ becomes present with His Nature, and we receive Him and approach Him with our own nature, fully immersed in Him. We come to

[4] Robert Cardinal Sarah, *The Power of Silence* (Ignatius Press, 2017), 226.

[5] See Saint Irenaeus, *Adv. haeres.* 3, 19, 1: *PG* 7/1, 939.

meet Him, allowing Him to sanctify us, and in doing so, we ourselves become a glorification of God.

Catholic worship in its millennial tradition—unchangeable in its essence—has always been open to different cultural and artistic expressions, the legitimate ones, over time. It has not been limited to an exclusive or closed cultural tradition in response to the God who seeks man. The legitimacy or not of the art to be used or the music to be performed depends accordingly on their source, on their origin. "Inculturation is not the canonization of a local culture or the decision to settle in that culture at the risk of absolutizing it. Inculturation is an epiphany of the Lord, who breaks into the most intimate recesses of our being."[6]

As I have said before, while the integration of human culture is important, it must never be the primary consideration. Instead, it should be integrated as a consequence of our participation in Christ's divine worship. We first experience this participation through baptism, when we become members of Christ's Body. With Christ as our High Priest, every liturgical celebration is truly a participation in His divine worship. Therefore, liturgical inculturation should flow from and be subordinate to our primary participation in Christ's divine worship, rather than being the central focus of the liturgy itself. When properly implemented, inculturation is always grounded in the essential truths of the faith, ensuring that we remain faithful to the tradition we have received, even as we seek new ways to express the eternal truths of the Gospel. Indeed, it is a powerful tool for evangelization, allowing the faith to penetrate ever more deeply into human culture, which in turn reflects the beauty of God's creation.

[6] Sarah, *Power of Silence*, 226.

*The Church's missionary efforts have sometimes been criticized as a form of religious and cultural colonization from Europe of countries throughout the world. How should we understand inculturation in light of these accusations of religious and cultural imperialism?*

We must never lose sight of the fact that the Church has a missionary identity: Just as the living Father sent Jesus into the world to save it, Christ Himself sent the Apostles to go forth into the whole world (see Jn 6:57), preaching salvation and baptizing every nation, every culture, and every person. This great commission is at the very heart of who we are as Christians. The Church has always sought to evangelize cultures, to sanctify what is true, good, and beautiful in them and to purify what is not. This process of evangelization necessarily involves a degree of inculturation. We see examples throughout history, from the early Church's use of Greek philosophical concepts to express theological truths, to the incorporation of artistic traditions in religious art and architecture.

Despite the fact that there are sadly many historical examples of members of the Church abusing the dignity and trust of indigenous peoples, we must still take Christ's command seriously today. We cannot allow past wrongs, or the fear of being misunderstood or criticized, to prevent the Church from fulfilling her apostolic mission to preach the Gospel and to baptize all nations. We must never be afraid to evangelize and to "do good for all men" (Gal 6:10). The sacraments, which the Church shares with every person and with every culture, were instituted by Christ for the salvation of the world. And the religious and cultural traditions surrounding the sacraments, especially the musical tradition of the Church, the Church likewise shares with all people for their spiritual nourishment and edification.

*For positive examples of inculturation in missionary activity we might look to Saints Cyril and Methodius, who translated the Church's liturgy into Slavonic in the ninth century, or the early Jesuits in North America, who translated and adapted parts of the liturgy for their Native American missions. How do these examples of liturgical inculturation differ from forms of inculturation that are to be rejected?*

Throughout the Church's history, missionaries have always learned the local languages so that they might effectively preach the Gospel and evangelize disparate nations. Nevertheless, when we approach the most sacred aspects of our faith, the celebration of the sacraments, the Church has nearly always communicated the sacredness of the mysteries by preserving the use of sacred languages to greater and lesser degrees. When the liturgy was first translated into Latin in the early Church, she retained the Hebrew words "Amen" and "Alleluia". These words were not "canceled" in favor of Latin. And so today, with Latin being the sacred language of the Roman Church, we must not cancel our traditions and traditional expressions of faith in favor of making everything new for each culture or even each generation.

In the process of catechesis, we must employ symbols, expressions, images, and popular elements that cater to the needs of those being evangelized, leading them toward Christ and conversion. But when praying or celebrating the liturgy, our primary focus should be on offering the best of ourselves to God. And to understand what that is, we must learn from the Church's cultural traditions that have developed around the liturgy over the centuries—the expressions, the symbols, and the music that have developed in the heart of the Church. In fact, these distinctive and traditional symbols of Christianity often have the benefit of being universally understood across diverse cultures, whether in India, Asia, Europe, or the Americas. The Church must indeed have great prudence and exercise caution when incorporating local expressions and symbols into the liturgy, as they may have different meanings to different tribes or peoples. I recall an instance when the Episcopal Conference of Latin America suggested removing the Agnus Dei from the liturgy, claiming that most people did not understand its meaning. However, eliminating the Agnus Dei would be tantamount to canceling the scriptures, as the words "Agnus Dei" were spoken by John the Baptist himself. The Agnus Dei is a universal expression, whereas replacing it with an Amazonian sign would only have meaning for a specific group of people. The symbol of the Lamb is present in the book of Genesis all the way to the Book of Revelation: "Worthy is the Lamb who was slain, to receive power and wealth and wisdom and might and honor and glory and blessing!" (Rev 5:12). "I saw no temple in the city, for its temple is the Lord God the Almighty and the Lamb. And the city has no need of sun or moon to shine upon it, for the glory of God is its light, and its lamp is the Lamb. By its light shall the nations walk; and the kings of the earth shall bring their glory into it" (Rev 21:22–24).

Inculturation is a very delicate process when it comes to understanding and communicating the Gospel message throughout the world. Over the centuries, the Church has developed a culture of sacred symbols and sacred music that are part of her tradition and identity. And many of these symbols come directly from Scripture: bread and wine, incense, and the offering of sacrifice. We must not cut ourselves off from our roots because they feel foreign or unfamiliar to us, or we risk cutting ourselves off from the Old and New Testaments and creating a new religion that is a religion of man.

*Inculturation, then, should not be understood as merely an effort of cultural inclusion within the liturgy?*

The liturgy is about God! It is not a celebration of man, or the place to promote any specific culture. Rather, it is the place where man encounters the Divine, and where the culture of man is baptized and raised to the height of the Divine. We must learn how to pray, and to do this we must ask the Church to teach us, just as the disciples asked our Lord. We must adapt ourselves to the liturgy, and not the liturgy to ourselves. It requires humility and a disciplining of our passions to truly and deeply pray the Our Father and to pray through the liturgical rites of the Church. But if we truly desire to learn how to pray, Our Lord will guide us. I wrote about this in *The Power of Silence*:

> Inculturation is not the canonization of a local culture or the decision to settle in that culture at the risk of absolutizing it. Inculturation is an epiphany of the Lord, who breaks into the most intimate recesses of our being. . . . It is not essentially accomplished by the utilization of local languages, Latin American instruments and music, African dances or African or Asian rites and symbols in the liturgy and the sacraments. Inculturation is God descending and entering into the life, the moral conduct, the cultures and customs of men so as to free them from sin and introduce them into the Trinitarian life.[7]

*How should the Church go about affirming what is good in various cultures while also sharing with them the gifts of her own cultural and liturgical traditions, especially in regard to sacred music?*

The Church's approach to inculturation, which has been a part of her journey for two millennia, is not about imposing

[7] Ibid., 226–27.

a culture or a particular cultural expression onto the liturgy but rather allowing the noble aspects of a culture to be incorporated into the liturgy in a way that both respects that culture and affirms the universal nature of our worship. This approach ensures that the liturgy remains a unifying force within the Church, transcending local and cultural boundaries. It's not about Africanizing or Europeanizing the liturgy, but about bringing local expressions into the broader tradition of the Church. Whether in Guinea, France, or Fiji, the liturgy should be unmistakably Catholic, part of the universal Church, a celebration of our shared faith rather than a faith that is divided by cultural identities. For instance, the *Messe Royale* composed by Henri du Mont in the Gregorian chant style is a beautiful expression of a distinctly French tradition of sacred music that is in harmony with the spirit of the liturgy and that has become part of the musical tradition of the Church. An African setting of the Mass ordinary that reflects African musicality can be just as enriching, provided it also maintains the spirit and integrity of the liturgy. However, this is often not what we witness in the Church today. As I said in a homily in Senegal in December 2023:

> We are witnessing today, especially in the West, a dismantling of the values of faith and piety . . . and a destruction of the forms of the mass. We work to sprinkle the liturgy with African and Asian elements, thus distorting the Paschal mystery that we celebrate. We place so much emphasis on these cultural elements that our celebrations sometimes last six hours. Our liturgies are often too banal and too noisy, too African and less Christian.[8]

[8] Rédaction Africanews with AFP, "Senegal: Cardinal Sarah Deplores a Distortion of Catholic Worship", *Africanews*, December 5, 2023, updated August 13, 2024, https://www.africanews.com/2023/12/05/senegal-cardinal-sarah-deplores-a-distortion-of-catholic-worship/.

True inculturation recognizes and affirms whatever is sacred and noble in a culture, as long as it is worthy to be "brought into the temple" and not contrary to the Gospel. However, bringing elements like drums and dancing from festivals into the Church would be a profanation of the sacred. Even in pagan religions, dancing is not typically part of the ritual offering of sacrifice. The people sit and listen silently while the priest addresses the deities and makes the offering on their behalf. Bringing dancing into the celebration of the Holy Mass is utterly useless in helping people to pray. While liturgical dancing sometimes occurs in Africa today, in my experience, this is not how Africans authentically communicate with God. It is not genuine inculturation.

When speaking of Gregorian chant and other forms of sacred music that have developed within the Church's tradition, we must not be afraid to share these gifts with the universal Church, as they truly belong to all Christians. However, we must also recognize that the Church's musical tradition is alive and never "complete" or "finished"—otherwise it runs the risk of becoming an ossified relic, a mere celebration of the past. Many of the Church's most treasured hymns were composed by saints and theologians who, inspired by their encounter with Christ, created new works of art and music for His glory. In regard to new compositions of sacred music, the Church today should certainly not discourage composers from this, but they must first learn to understand and to love the Church's musical tradition if they hope to add to her riches. The legitimate artistic desire for creative self-expression is not sufficient for a composition to be suitable for the liturgy; it must truly be sacred in all its elements. Liturgical music should help us enter spiritually into the encounter with God in the liturgy, not merely be artistically or emotionally cathartic for the composer or the performer.

## *Dancing Before the Lord*

*Some argue that the incorporation of dancing into the liturgy has a biblical justification, pointing to the passage in 2 Samuel where King David danced before the Ark of the Covenant. How should we understand this passage? Does it support the use of dance as a valid expression of liturgical worship?*

It is important to note that in the passage from 2 Samuel, as the Ark of the Covenant was being brought in procession, David was dancing in the street, not within the Temple itself. And this is the only passage where it is said that David was dancing; the account is not repeated elsewhere in the Old Testament. And let me add a very important point: The unique example of our liturgical prayer and the unique Teacher of how we should pray is Jesus Christ: "He was praying in a certain place, and when he ceased, one of his disciples said to him: Lord, teach us to pray, as John taught his disciples" (Lk 11:1). We must avoid a noisy, agitated, very rhythmical, and dancing way of praying! It is not the way of Christ. It is entertainment, an amusement, recreation.

The Church has always distinguished between the liturgical worship that takes place within the sacred space of the church and the popular festivities that cultures develop to celebrate religious holidays. While these festivities can sometimes be closely related to liturgical celebrations, as in the case of processions, the Church has always reinforced the distinction between liturgical celebrations inside the church and religious festivities outside of the church.

The appropriateness of dancing during Holy Mass, particularly as happens in Africa, is a serious matter that requires careful reflection by the African bishops. When we pray in the liturgy, we must imitate our Lord, who teaches us how to pray. The Scriptures never describe Jesus dancing while praying—or the Virgin Mary, our Mater and Magistra, or the Apostles. While we might speculate that Christ danced at the wedding feast in Cana, this would have been a nuptial celebration separate from the worship of the Temple. The Church has historically allowed for certain instruments and expressions of joy to be used in processions outside of the church building, while maintaining a more solemn and restrained atmosphere within the liturgy itself. There is no contradiction in this; it is a matter of recognizing the distinct nature and purpose of these different spheres of religious life. We must contemplate the example of Christ at prayer, where He "withdrew from [his disciples] about a stone's throw, and knelt down and prayed" (Lk 22:41), and also Christ praying on the cross offering His sacrifice to the Father. The Holy Mass is the memorial of Christ's sacrifice on the cross, this painful but beautiful moment of salvation. It is not a celebration of human activity or human artistry, but a solemn remembrance of Christ's redeeming death. Inculturation cannot change the fundamental reality of Jesus' death on the cross for our redemption. Cultures must not transform the Eucharistic liturgy into a chaotic spectacle that obscures this essential truth. If we try to be creative with the liturgy and overload our Eucharistic celebrations with too many African and cultural elements, we will swamp, damage, and destroy the sacredness of the Eucharistic Sacrifice. We have nothing to invent! We must keep what we received from the Sacred Tradition and from our fathers in faith. It is the same in regard to theological research. In an interview in 1996, Joseph Ratzinger characterized his own approach to theology in terms of "ressourcement" or a "thinking together with the great masters of the faith":

> I have never tried to create a system of my own, an individual theology. What is specific, if you want to call it that, is that I simply want to think in communion with the faith of the Church, and that means above all to think in communion with the great thinkers of the faith. The aim is not an isolated theology that I draw out of myself but one that opens as widely as possible into the common intellectual pathway of the faith. For this reason exegesis was always very important. I couldn't imagine a purely philosophical theology. The point of departure is first of all the word. That we believe the word of God, that we try really to get to know and understand it, and then, as I said, to think it together with the great masters of the faith. This gives my theology a somewhat biblical character and also bears the stamp of the Fathers, especially Augustine.[9]

Ultimately, the question is not whether God loves the cultures of His people—of course He does. God loves everyone. But He does not love everything that they do, and not everything they do and create is worthy of His temple. The Church's task, acting as the good shepherd, is to discern which cultural elements can be harmoniously incorporated into her worship in a way that preserves its sacred character and deepens the faith of her flock. Dancing may have a legitimate place in religious festivities and celebrations, but liturgical celebrations must remain focused on the solemn memorial of Christ's Paschal Mystery, which is the source of our salvation.

[9] Joseph Cardinal Ratzinger, *Salt of the Earth: Christianity and the Catholic Church at the End of the Millennium*, trans. Adrian Walker (Ignatius Press, 1997), 66.

*Perhaps we can point to some positive examples of inculturation throughout the Church's history to serve as a guide. The Pantheon in Rome, for instance, demonstrates how even a pagan temple can be "baptized" and transformed for sacred use as a Christian church. And the flowers that adorn churches are an example of utilizing the beauty of nature found in local surroundings to communicate the spiritual beauty of the liturgy. In the realm of music, composers like Sir James MacMillan come to mind for me, since he has a distinct musical language that reflects the musical traditions of his culture, drawing upon them to create beautiful new compositions of sacred music. His sacred music has a distinctly Scottish flavor with its rhythms and melodies, yet it remains clearly sacred in character. The Mass of the Americas by Frank La Rocca is another example of drawing from traditional Mexican folk music to create a unique expression of the faith that is rooted in the cultural heritage of the Americas. How might these examples be different from the imposition of the music of a culture upon the liturgy?*

It is true that the Second Vatican Council encouraged a greater openness to cultural adaptation in the liturgy, but always in a way that adorns the liturgy and reinforces its sacred character, rather than a mere celebration of culture. The Church welcomes and celebrates cultural expressions such as the ones you described, as they are utilized in a way that serves and enhances the sacred character of the liturgy while respecting the cultures that they represent.

The Church also welcomes a much wider range of religious and cultural celebrations outside of the liturgy, where they still have a great importance in forming faith and leading the faithful to understand and participate in the sacred liturgy better. In Provence, for example, there is a beautiful tradition of crafting nativity scenes that distinctly reflect the Provençal culture. These crèches are a wonderful example of inculturation, allowing the mystery of the Incarnation to be expressed in a way that resonates with the people. However, it is important to remember that this practice remains distinct from the liturgy itself. The crèche is not brought into the sanctuary, and the songs sung around it are not the same as those sung at Christmas Mass.

The same principle applies to other cultural traditions surrounding the liturgical seasons. There may be special foods, decorations, or customs that mark feast days in different parts of the world. A country's celebration of its patronal saint's feast day often provides a unified cultural celebration that can bring people into a deeper knowledge and appreciation of the saint and their holiness of life. This diversity of traditions can be a beautiful expression of the Church's universality, though when they are divorced from their religious character, they become mere occasions of indulgence and even blasphemous, as is unfortunately the case with many cultural celebrations of holy days, such as that of Saint Patrick.

In the liturgy itself, we must preserve a unity that transcends cultural differences, whether in Africa, Asia, Europe, or the Americas. The celebration of the sacraments is what binds us all together as one body in Christ. This is why the Council, while encouraging a degree of cultural adaptation, also affirmed the primacy of Gregorian chant and the pipe organ as the proper music of the Roman Rite. These forms have a universally sacred quality that allows them to resonate with Catholics of all cultures. They are not tied to a particular time or place but rather lift our hearts and minds to God in a perennial way. Of course, this does not mean there is no room for other musical forms in the liturgy, as you mentioned in your question. The Council left open the possibility for other instruments and styles to be admitted, provided they are truly suitable for sacred use.

In all of this, we must remember that the purpose of the liturgy is the worship of God and the edification of the faithful, and we must be discerning in this regard, not simply making concessions and adapting the liturgy to popular tastes and preferences that compromise its sacred character. Universality means that what is truly beautiful and good in one culture can transcend cultural boundaries and be beautiful and good for the Church universal.

# 8

# THE SENSE OF THE SACRED

PETER CARTER: *Your Eminence, we have been discussing the use of the vernacular and inculturation in the liturgy. Both are areas in the liturgical reform that began with solid principles and a noble purpose; but in practice, as you have said, they have frequently led to misunderstanding and distortion of the purpose and nature of the liturgy. Too often, people approach the Mass as they might a concert or a lecture, seeking an interesting and edifying experience to uplift their soul. However, this attitude stands in stark contrast to the profound reverence and awe they should have when participating in the sacred worship of almighty God. It seems to me that the manner in which the vernacular and inculturation have been applied to the liturgy have greatly contributed to the loss of the sense of the sacred that we often experience in the Church's liturgy today. How would you describe the essential qualities of a liturgy that is truly imbued with a sense of the sacred?*

ROBERT CARDINAL SARAH: The loss of the sense of the sacred is at the heart of the liturgical crisis that we are experiencing in many parts of the Church today. When we approach the liturgy primarily as a human creation, as a human act, subject to our own preferences and agendas, we risk losing sight of its true nature as an act of worship offered by Christ Himself to the Father, in which we are privileged to participate by virtue of our baptism.

Consider Moses' encounter with God in the burning bush on Mount Sinai. Here we see an example of how we should approach the divine presence made manifest in the liturgy. Moses does not assert himself or his people, but rather humbly surrenders himself to the mystery of the living God. He takes off his sandals, recognizing that he is standing on holy ground, and he allows himself to be drawn into an intimate conversation with the Divine, mysteriously made present in the burning bush. Moses was transformed by his encounter with the Lord, and his face remained radiant, showing forth the glory of God to the Israelites. This, then, is the same disposition we must cultivate when we come to worship: a humble and reverent openness to the transforming power of God's presence. We do not come to the liturgy to assert ourselves or to represent our peoples or cultures, but rather to be conformed more perfectly to Christ, allowing His grace to refashion us in His image.

The human elements of the liturgy are meant to be channels of God's grace, not a mere celebration of human genius. When we allow the external signs and symbols of the liturgy to become our focus, we are making them a barrier between man and God rather than a channel of God's grace to man. It is easier to filter our experience of God through human personalities—the reader, the priest, the musicians—than to allow ourselves to be confronted directly by His presence. If we take seriously the Word of God, then we will acknowledge that it is indeed terrifying at times, because it calls us out of our complacency and demands a total conversion of our lives to God. Instead, we must learn to surrender ourselves to the transformative power of the sacred rites themselves, allowing them to lift us out of our mundane existence into the very life of God. This requires a very real death to self, and a willingness to let go of our own preferences and ideas in order to be reborn in Christ.

*It seems, then, that the priest, and even all who have liturgical roles, should not draw attention to themselves, but rather show forth Christ through their role in the liturgy. How should priests and all liturgical ministers, including musicians, cultivate this sense of hiddenness and self-effacement while fulfilling their unique roles and obligations?*

The priest and liturgical ministers are called to a profound humility and forgetfulness of self. They are not there to showcase their own personality or to entertain the congregation, but rather to be a living icon of Christ, the eternal High Priest. Like John the Baptist, they must always point beyond themselves to the Lamb of God, saying. "He must increase, but I must decrease" (Jn 3:30).

For the priest to cultivate this sense of hiddenness, he must first and foremost be a man of deep prayer, learning to surrender himself completely to Christ. When he celebrates the sacred rites, he must do so with a profound reverence and attention, careful not to impose his own will or to add anything of his own, but rather to be a faithful steward of the mysteries entrusted to him. Every gesture, every word, must be imbued with a sense of the sacred, reflecting the utter seriousness of Christ's sacrifice, the same sacrifice he offers on the altar. When the priest proclaims the Gospel, he becomes the very mouthpiece of God, speaking not his own words but the words of eternal life. This responsibility should fill him with a holy fear and awe, as he is the instrument through which the face of Christ must shine forth unobstructed. His whole being should be oriented toward the cross and the altar, the twin poles of the Christian mystery, drawing the gaze of the faithful toward the sacrificial love that is the heart of our faith. In this way, the priest becomes a living sacrament of Christ's presence in the world, a sign and instrument of the holiness to which all the baptized are called.

*This sacramental understanding of the liturgy, in which the earthly realities of words, gestures, and material elements become instruments of divine grace, seems to be at the heart of a truly sacred worship. In contrast, it seems that a more didactic or rationalistic approach to the liturgy can obscure this sense of mystery, since it prioritizes intellectual comprehension and even a sort of academic formation. How can we recover a more integrated, holistic vision of the liturgy as a work of God in which we are invited to participate?*

The liturgy, as the Second Vatican Council teaches, is indeed the "font" and "summit" of the Christian life,[1] the privileged locus where we encounter personally and face-to-face the living God and are gradually transformed into His likeness. To reduce this profound mystery to either a mere text to be recited, a didactic exercise, or even an emotive experience is to rob it of its true power and beauty. Liturgy that lacks beauty and fails to engage the whole person, body and soul, will quickly become monotonous and fail to lift us out of our mundane cares into God's presence.

As Pope Benedict XVI reminded us in his apostolic exhortation *Sacramentum caritatis*, the liturgy is fundamentally God's work, not our own.

> Since the eucharistic liturgy is essentially an *actio Dei* which draws us into Christ through the Holy Spirit, its basic structure is not something within our power to change, nor can it be held hostage by the latest trends. Here too Saint Paul's irrefutable statement applies: "no one can lay any foundation other than the one that has been laid, which is Jesus Christ" (1 Cor 3:11). Again it is the Apostle of the Gen-

[1] Vatican Council II, Constitution on the Sacred Liturgy *Sacrosanctum concilium* (December 4, 1963), no. 10.

> tiles who assures us that, with regard to the Eucharist, he is presenting not his own teaching but what he himself has received (cf. 1 Cor 11:23). The celebration of the Eucharist implies and involves the living Tradition.[2]

The liturgy is not a human invention or a platform for our own self-expression, but rather a gift received in faith and humility. The art of celebrating the liturgy well, therefore, consists not in drawing attention to ourselves or in trying to "make things interesting", but rather in allowing the innate beauty and power of the rites to shine forth, unobscured by our own personalities or agendas. This beauty, as Pope Benedict XVI also notes, does not necessarily require grandiose architecture or magnificent artistry, but it does demand an integral harmony and fittingness in all the elements of the celebration:

> The truest beauty is the love of God, who definitively revealed himself to us in the paschal mystery.
>
> The beauty of the liturgy is part of this mystery; it is a sublime expression of God's glory and, in a certain sense, a glimpse of heaven on earth. The memorial of Jesus' redemptive sacrifice contains something of that beauty which Peter, James and John beheld when the Master, making his way to Jerusalem, was transfigured before their eyes (cf. Mk 9:2). Beauty, then, is not mere decoration, but rather an essential element of the liturgical action, since it is an attribute of God himself and his revelation. These considerations should make us realize the care which is needed, if the liturgical action is to reflect its innate splendour.[3]

The music, ceremonies, art, and vestments form a whole, a rich feast for the senses that speaks to worshipers in diverse

[2] Benedict XVI, post-synodal apostolic exhortation *Sacramentum caritatis* (The Sacrament of Charity) (February 22, 2007), no. 37.

[3] Ibid., no. 35.

ways. The rising incense symbolizing our prayers carried heavenward, the Scriptures proclaimed in song, the visual splendor of the rites—all these draw us into the mystery of Christ's saving work and enrich our encounter with Him. But it is also not a platform for showcasing our own talents and abilities. Any view of liturgy that places the artistic or personal expression of man at the center is fundamentally flawed. Of course, personal piety and devotions have their place, but these must flow from and lead back to the sacred liturgy, never eclipsing it. For the liturgy is not about us—our choices, our feelings, our favorite prayers, or our favorite hymns. It is about our desperate need for salvation in Christ. The liturgical prayer breaks through our illusions of self-sufficiency, inviting us to "follow the Lamb wherever he goes" (Rev 14:4). When we acknowledge this, we can begin to appreciate the liturgy for what it truly is. We must approach the altar with the humility of the publican in Christ's parable, beating our breasts and crying out, "God, be merciful to me a sinner!" (Lk 18:14). Only when we recognize how radically we depend on God's mercy can we rightly offer ourselves with Christ to the Father.

Some approved translations of the Mass obscure this understanding of the liturgy as a plea for salvation. Where the prayer before Communion evoked the Roman centurion's need for salvation, declaring, "Lord, I am not worthy that you should enter under my roof, but only say the word and *my soul* shall be healed" (see Lk 18:8), some translations substitute the first person pronoun, saying instead "and *I* shall be healed". This was corrected in the new English translation of the Mass, but it is still a problem in many other translations. In fact, this seemingly small alteration touches on the very meaning of our participation in the liturgy. It is not about a transformation in our temporal, earthly lives, but about the redemption of our eternal souls. Jesus indeed came to save his people from their sins (see Mt 1:21; Lk 7:50). Losing sight of this truth can lead to a temporal, worldly, and horizontal understanding of worship that places us and our perceived needs at the center.

## *Using the Liturgy for Particular Charisms*

*In a similar vein, some Catholics seek to promote particular initiatives or charisms through the liturgy, as a means either of evangelization or of academic formation in the Scriptures or of music and the arts. Is there a danger in instrumentalizing the liturgy to promote a particular cause, or approaching the liturgy as a means to "get something useful" out of the experience?*

The danger of falling into utilitarian attitudes regarding the liturgy always exists. But the liturgy is the worshipful encounter of the Church with the living God. It can have no other purpose. In his apostolic exhortation *Evangelii gaudium*, Pope Francis cites Pope Saint John Paul II:

> It is worth remembering that "the liturgical proclamation of the word of God, especially in the eucharistic assembly, is not so much a time for meditation and catechesis as a dialogue between God and his people, a dialogue in which the great deeds of salvation are proclaimed and the demands of the covenant are continually restated."...
>
> The homily cannot be a form of entertainment like those presented by the media, yet it does need to give life and meaning to the celebration. It is a distinctive genre, since it is preaching situated within the framework of a liturgical

celebration; hence it should be brief and avoid taking on the semblance of a speech or a lecture.[4]

It is a serious deviation from the Church's understanding of the liturgy to try to promote a particular person, cause, or culture through it, however noble the intention. Sacred music, and all of sacred art, serves as a humble handmaid of the liturgy, expressing its mysterious meaning in ways that we can understand and relate to, but always in the effort to show forth the beauty and magnificence of God, not the genius or cleverness of man. All art and music acquire a holiness when they lead us to God, who is at the center of the liturgy.

## *Technology in the Liturgy*

*We see everywhere how our modern culture demands immediate responses and satisfaction, and how we have grown accustomed to it through the development of technology. You discussed in* The Power of Silence, *your Eminence, how in the modern world our lives are filled with constant stimulation and noise, never allowing us to experience the void of silence. And when we do encounter silence, we are left feeling uncomfortable, forced to confront ourselves, but it is through the silence of prayer we come to face God directly. The utilization of technology in the liturgy is promoted by some as a means to engage and participate in the liturgy, though not usually in the manner in which you describe liturgical participation. But can technology be used in a way that facilitates true participation, or do modern technologies, like phones and screen projectors, tend to contribute*

[4] Francis, apostolic exhortation *Evangelii gaudium* (The Joy of the Gospel) (November 24, 2013), nos. 137–38, quoting John Paul II, apostolic letter *Dies Domini* (On Keeping the Lord's Day Holy) (May 31, 1998), no. 41.

*toward a desacralization of the liturgy, keeping us in a state of superficial stimulation and passive distraction?*

Recording videos on phones is sadly very common in Masses, especially during moments of joy as in processions or during particularly beautiful music. However, our internalization of the moment and our participation in the sacred mysteries is ignored when we try to capture and preserve it. This is spectating, not participation! Christ is ignored, not adored! Any technology that creates a barrier to participation should be excluded from the liturgy, as it pulls us away from the awesome reality of divine worship. While the projector screen can sometimes aid participation in large liturgical celebrations, it can also sometimes be counterproductive in truly entering into the sacred rites, as the focus can easily be drawn to the screen where we watch the liturgy unfold like a movie, separate from ourselves. Utilizing these screens to show the texts or music of the liturgy most often becomes a distraction to true interior participation through the intrusive and didactic nature of the medium. A booklet or a hymnal is often much more discreet and allow a more personal engagement with the technological medium. But we do not even need these forms of technology to truly participate, and the utilization of technology should never become an end in and of itself—merely using it because we can. All technology must be at the service of the liturgy and must never contribute to a loss of its sacredness.

*In relation to music, I have noticed from personal experience that it is much easier to sing from the heart while also singing from memory. I encourage this with my choirs as much as possible, as we sing the same chants of the Mass ordinary week to week, throughout the liturgical seasons. The eyes can often be a distraction from real music making when they are constantly looking at and "hiding behind" their music scores. When singers are not worried about singing the correct notes, they are free to let the music be an expression of their hearts.*

*During the Covid lockdown, people obviously could not physically be present at Mass, so many places broadcast or live-streamed their Masses. What are your thoughts of watching the Mass on the television or computer?*

This was a difficult period for the whole Church, a time we all suffered through together. In exceptional circumstances like this, or if one is ill or infirm, it is better to watch a video of the Mass than to do nothing at all. But this must truly be an exception. Christ instituted sacraments for the Church—physical symbols through which we receive His grace, and with the Eucharist, Christ Himself. Since we are made of body and soul, we cannot fully participate in the liturgy if we remain physically absent. Because of this, we must be physically present for the celebration of the Eucharist, as in a symbolic and spiritual way, we die physically with Christ on the altar. Just as a husband and wife must be together to fully express their love for each other, so too must we be physically united with Christ who is made present in the Mass.

*I have noticed that one effect of the lockdown period was that some live-streamed Masses not only connected people with the liturgy, but provided opportunities for instruction in how beautiful the liturgy can be if imbued with a proper* ars celebrandi. *What comes to mind for me are the live-streamed Masses of Saint John Cantius in Chicago. Nevertheless, the instructional aspect to recorded Masses serves a very different purpose from the liturgy itself.*

Yes, technology can be utilized well for instruction and formation, but it can never replace being fully present in the liturgy, because our participation is with body and soul.

Otherwise, we risk truly becoming spectators of the Mass, turning the Mass into entertainment for our own enjoyment and pleasure. This betrays both the meaning of the Mass and our participation in it as Christians.

## *Pastoral Accommodations in the Liturgy*

*Just as the Mass is not a television program, it seems that planning liturgies should not be approached in the same way that a business might plan an event—trying to grow their audience and increase their revenues.*

The Church is not a business trying to drive sales. And the sacred liturgy is not a mere human celebration with earthly ends, offered for our pleasure or edification like a concert or lecture. No, it is something infinitely greater! It is the very sacrifice of Christ Himself, offered to the Father for the salvation of the world. Our approach to planning or participating in the liturgy, then, must never be reduced to a question of "What does this do for me?" or "How does it make me feel?" Rather, we must always ask, with reverence and humility, "What is God doing for us in this sacred action?" and "How can I unite myself more perfectly with Christ's sacrifice?"

If we celebrate the liturgy with true sacredness, it will indeed make us holy—not because we happen to like the priest or the music, but because we have encountered the living God. And it is this encounter that has completely changed my life and enables me to say, like Saint Paul: "For to me to live is Christ, and to die is gain" (Phil 1:21), and "I have been crucified with Christ; it is no longer I who live, but Christ who lives in me" (Gal 2:20). Evaluating the efficacy of the liturgy by mere sociological data, the number of compliments we receive, or the whims of popular taste betrays a lack of faith in its divine power. We must approach the sacred mysteries with humility and patience, trusting that God's grace will bear fruit in His own time.

*It is my understanding that prior to 1953, the Church usually permitted Masses to be celebrated only in the morning. This kept intact the integrity of the liturgical hours when they were celebrated throughout the day. However, since then, evening Masses have become a common practice in the Roman Rite to help enable the faithful participate when they otherwise might not be able to. Do you think this change in liturgical practice has been spiritually beneficial for the Church?*

The Church sanctifies all the hours of the day by offering them to God in her liturgical worship. This was traditionally done through the celebration of the Divine Office, from Matins in the middle of the night, now most commonly celebrated as the Office of Readings, all the way to Compline, the Church's night prayer. The Mass is the greatest of the Church's liturgies, as it is a celebration of the very sacrifice of Christ, in obedience to His command to "do this in remembrance of me" (Lk 22:19). While the change in allowing the Mass to be celebrated at any hour of the day has had some real fruit, it has also had some unintended consequences that have contributed to a misunderstanding of the Mass and its place in the Church's life. One consequence has been to diminish the importance of other liturgical hours in the hearts of the faithful, as many parishes today only offer the Mass to the exclusion of the public celebration of the Divine Office. The Divine Office is also the liturgy of the Church and is intended to be prayed publicly, not only privately, as if it were a religious devotion unique to priests and religious. Another unfortunate consequence has been to reinforce a form of legalism, viewing the obligation to attend Sunday Mass as something to check off a weekly to-do list, as if our duty to make holy the Lord's Day is merely to show up for a weekly meeting. It also betrays a consumerist mentality toward the liturgy, allowing it to be seen as a commodity available "on demand" like a twenty-four-hour restaurant, especially since modern society views faith as a predominantly private or social practice, secondary to business, sports, or even extra hours of sleep. This can easily develop into a casual attitude that says, "I'll go to Mass if I have the time", revealing a tragic lack of faith. There is certainly a danger if the Church's only response to this attitude is to move the Mass to the most convenient times in order to please people, as it betrays a defeatist attitude that puts the convenience of man above the glory of God. This is not to say that evening Masses should be stopped, but that we must form the faithful to truly understand what the Mass is and the fundamental importance it must have in our lives.

The fundamental question we must ask ourselves is, Who is God in my life? Does how I live my life communicate that He is truly the origin and goal of my existence, the one to whom I owe the totality of my being? If we recognize this truth, we will not begrudge the sacrifice of our time, energy, and other social obligations to be present at the appointed hour when the Church celebrates the sacred mysteries. We will hunger for the Eucharist as our essential sustenance, not treating it as a convenience that is dispensable.

*The Church also made an allowance for the Saturday evening Mass to fulfill the faithful's obligation to attend Mass on Sundays.*

Yes. The Church allowed this as a pastoral accommodation that was initially limited in scope, especially to accommodate those whose attendance on Sundays was onerous or impossible, such as those involved in healthcare or other essential services that would preclude their attendance at

Sunday Mass. But now, the Church allows all the faithful to fulfill their Sunday obligation by attending a Saturday evening Mass, regardless of their ability to attend Mass on Sundays. This expansive accommodation, I believe, has had grave consequences for the *sensus fidei*, diminishing the cultural appreciation of Sunday as a day that is truly set apart for God. What is really a tragedy in all this is that it is done for the mere convenience and satisfaction of man, not first for the glorification and honor of God. Sadly, in this way, even in the Catholic Church, man is first and God second. Man has taken the place of God.

Sunday, the day of the Resurrection, is meant to be kept holy, dedicated to worship and rest in the Lord. We must take God seriously when He asks us to keep holy the Lord's Day, this special day He consecrated through His Resurrection and that we celebrate as a weekly Easter of the Church! We must never prioritize our convenience over the Lord's command! Regardless of the busyness of our lives, the worship of the Creator is our first obligation as His creatures. The liturgy must truly be the "font" and "apex" not only of the life of the Church, but in the lives of each of her members. And when members of the Church are not able to attend Mass because of illness or obligation, they can still spiritually unite themselves to the Church's prayer. The priests and faithful should make efforts to maintain their relationship with the community of the Church, as the Church is a family who love one another and who suffer with one another.

## *Silence as an Expression of Reverence*

*There are times when conversation may be necessary in the church during some events such as wedding rehearsals and music rehearsals, though sometimes this devolves into casual behavior within the church.*

*Indeed, it is not uncommon in many Western countries for people to greet one another and talk freely to each other before or after the liturgy while still in the church. How should the faithful, who have no intention of being disrespectful, be taught how to be respectful and show proper reverence while in church?*

The festive atmosphere found at the end of the Sunday Mass is truly wonderful. Families, children, young and old, and the sacred ministers have come together as the people of God to rejoice in the Lord's Resurrection. The conclusion of the Holy Mass, following the "Ite missa est", marks Christ's definitive triumph over sin, death, and darkness as the message of hope for the world. In parish churches or cathedrals where the pipe organ is played, the joy is often expressed through the instrumental jubilation showing forth God's majesty and glory. However, even in the midst of this joyful fellowship, we must never forget that we are still in the house of God, a sacred space demanding a reverent demeanor and proper decorum. There is a maxim attributed to Saint Philip Neri that one should "never make a noise of any sort in the church, except of the greatest necessity". This is a simple and wonderful rule that helps to preserve the sense of sacredness that should pervade the holy temple of God at all times. Silence is truly a veil to the sacred, and when this silence is lost and filled with conversation, the veil of the temple is torn and replaced with the mundane cares of the day. Even when the church building is used for legitimate purposes outside of the liturgy itself, a general sense of reverence and respectful restraint should be maintained.

Before the Mass begins, the church should be filled with each person talking with God, not talking with one another! This personal prayer prepares our hearts to join in the liturgical and communal prayer of the Church. As the Mass begins, and the introit is chanted, the silence preceding it gives way to the singing of the psalms, announcing to the faithful that the celebration of sacred mysteries has begun, and inviting them to lift up their hearts to the Lord.

During his visit to Ostia in 1963, Pope Saint John XXIII was joyfully greeted by the faithful with thunderous applause as he entered the church. With graciousness for his warm welcome, he gently reproved them, reminding them that the church is the temple of God, and that while he was happy to see his children, "as soon as [the pope] sees his good children, he certainly does not clap his hands in their faces."[5] The Holy Father, guiding them as their shepherd, humbly directed their gaze beyond himself to the one whom he represented, Christ the Lord. Pope Benedict XVI also clearly taught that applause or celebratory cheering has no place within the Mass itself. He wrote, "Wherever applause breaks out in the liturgy because of some human achievement, it is a sure sign that the essence of liturgy has totally disappeared and been replaced by a kind of religious entertainment."[6]

The use of the organ in the liturgy also warrants reflection. This instrument, hailed by the Second Vatican Council as "the traditional musical instrument which adds a wonderful splendor to the Church's ceremonies and powerfully lifts up man's mind to God and to higher things",[7] has the capacity to express both peaceful meditation and majestic jubilation, particularly in the moments before and immediately following the liturgical celebrations. Its solemn tones can be harmoniously integrated into the liturgical prayer,

[5] Gregory DiPippo, "St John XXIII Asks the Faithful Not to Applaud in Church", *New Liturgical Movement*, July 27, 2014, https://www.newliturgicalmovement.org/2014/07/st-john-xxiii-asks-faithful-not-to.html.

[6] Joseph Cardinal Ratzinger, *The Spirit of the Liturgy* (Ignatius Press, 2000), 198.

[7] *Sacrosanctum concilium*, no. 120.

having the power to lift our minds and hearts to God. And yet, all too often, the organ is often put aside in favor of instruments more culturally familiar but less sacred, such as the guitar. As is all too common in western Europe, the organ's majestic voice is relegated to nonliturgical occasions, such as concerts or recitals.

At the blessing of a new organ at the Alte Kapelle in Regensburg, Pope Benedict XVI remarked, "The organ has always been considered, and rightly so, the king of musical instruments, because it takes up all the sounds of creation . . . and gives resonance to the fullness of human sentiments, from joy to sadness, from praise to lamentation. By transcending the merely human sphere, as all music of quality does, it evokes the divine. The organ's great range of timbre, from *piano* through to a thundering *fortissimo*, makes it an instrument superior to all others. It is capable of echoing and expressing all the experiences of human life. The manifold possibilities of the organ in some way remind us of the immensity and the magnificence of God."[8]

## *Liturgical Unity in a Diverse Church*

*Cultivating a liturgical life for a parish community can be a challenging task, especially in large churches that minister to different ethnic communities. How might unity be maintained in a parish that has multiple communities within it?*

I recognize that gathering ethnic communities together helps reinforce their ethnic unity and strengthens their cultural identity and mutual support. But I question whether these

[8] Pope Benedict XVI, Blessing of the New Organ in Regensburg's Alte Kapelle (September 13, 2006), https://www.vatican.va/content/benedict-xvi/en/speeches/2006/september/documents/hf_ben-xvi_spe_20060913_alte-kapelle-regensburg.html.

are the kind of communities Jesus Christ intended to build by dying on the cross. Did Jesus come to reinforce different ethnic communities? Was it not prophesied that Jesus was going to die for the nations—not only for the Jewish nation—and gather into one the dispersed children of God (see Jn 11:51–52)? Indeed there is no enmity between different ethnic groups in the Church. However, promoting Masses for Hispanic, Polish, Vietnamese, or Filipino communities is not building the Church, the Body of Christ, but creating distinctly human and cultural churches. Saint Paul reminds us:

> But now in Christ Jesus you who once were far off have been brought near in the blood of Christ. For he is our peace, who has made us both one, and has broken down the dividing wall of hostility, by abolishing in his flesh the law of commandments and ordinances, that he might create in himself one new man in place of the two, so making peace, and might reconcile us both to God in one body through the cross, thereby bringing the hostility to an end. (Eph 2:13–16)

I invite everybody to reflect profoundly on ethnic and cultural Masses, in the one Church of Jesus Christ, remembering that He said to us: "He who is not with me is against me, and he who does not gather with me scatters" (Mt 12:30; Lk 11:23).

The fragmentation of society is a reality of modern life, particularly in the West, and the Church ministers to her faithful despite this fragmentation, always seeking to unite a local community of believers with the universal community of the Church. The Eucharist, by its very nature, is meant to be a sacrament of unity, transcending all human divisions. As Saint Paul reminds us, in Christ "there is neither Jew nor Greek, there is neither slave nor free, there is neither male nor female; for you are all one in Christ Jesus" (Gal 3:28).

This fundamental unity should be reflected in the way we worship. While it may be pastorally beneficial to have certain Masses in different languages, we should not lose sight of the fact that Latin is a powerful sign and instrument of unity. Similarly, chanting the ordinary parts of the Mass together—the Kyrie, Gloria, Credo, Sanctus, and Agnus Dei—using the simple and beautiful Gregorian chant melodies, immediately connects us with the universal Church across time and space. Imagine the witness to a parish's unity in Christ if, at the installation of a new pastor, the entire parish could join as one voice in singing the Credo in Latin, rather than having the profession of faith divided into several different languages.

Multiculturalism may be a reality in the world today, but in the celebration of the liturgy we should not seek to reinforce separate cultural identities but be united in our faith as Christians, freely embracing the sacred culture of the Church's liturgical tradition.

*There is a modern phenomenon of having themed Masses for specific groups of people: a children's Mass, a teen Mass, etc.—even LGBT Masses in some places. Where this is done, it seems to be done as an effort to minister to the different groups of the parish through these themed celebrations of the Mass. Is this pastoral approach valid or appropriate?*

The Holy Sacrifice of the Mass is not a celebration of or for any particular group of people. Much less is it a celebration of sexual inclinations or sinful behaviors that some people have embraced as part of their identity. Wherever this latter type of celebration occurs, it is truly sacrilegious, a profanation of the Holy of Holies. The "theme" of every Mass should be the worship of God. Christ offered Himself for the salvation of all men, not a particular group, so when the Church liturgically celebrates Christ's sacrifice in the

Mass, it is likewise for the whole Church, not for a particular group. Celebrating regularly and systematically the Holy Mass particularly for a specific group of people is indeed destroying the paschal mystery of Jesus Christ. I think that such religious practices are distortions of the Holy Mass and far removed from what Jesus intended by dying on the cross. Therefore, I ask pastors especially to reflect deeply on this. Certain groups may legitimately require special pastoral care, but this is properly done outside of the liturgy and without detracting from the integrity of the liturgy. The prayers of the Mass certainly change according to the feast, season, or particular occasion that is being celebrated, such as a wedding or a funeral Mass. The Church also allows for special blessings and petitions to be offered for particular groups within the context of the Mass—the honoring of wedding or ordination anniversaries, for example, or the blessing of firefighters or doctors on the feast of their patrons. Even with these blessings, though, the essence of the liturgy remains the same. It is not transformed or distorted into something else than what it is to appease a certain group. This would be sacrilegious.

The idea of having special Masses for children is nonsense, as this both infantilizes the children and desacralizes the liturgy. The Mass is offered for the whole Church, not just for adults or children, and to believe that the manner in which the Church offers the Mass is inaccessible to children betrays a lack of understanding both of participation and of the Mass itself. Much children's music is simplistic and puerile, perhaps appropriate for home or school but not for the dignified worship of God. Instead of having the liturgy adapted to cater to them, children should be immersed in the splendor and beauty of the Church's liturgy, sacred music, and art! If their parents and teachers teach them patiently and diligently, they will gradually learn to understand, appreciate, and love the liturgy celebrated "in the beauty of holiness". The same is true for teenagers and young adults. All of the baptized can fully participate in the liturgy, each according to their own capacity. We continually return to the theme that liturgical music, and indeed every aspect of the Church's liturgy, must possess a universal character—a transcendent beauty that lifts us out of our narrow, earthly horizons and into the presence of God.

When we celebrate the liturgy in a manner that places undue emphasis on local customs, particular languages, or specific "target audiences", we risk reducing it to a purely horizontal, anthropocentric exercise. The danger is that we can end up celebrating ourselves—our own cultures, identities, and accomplishments—rather than the salvific work of Jesus. What should be most important in our lives that we celebrate is not what we possess or what we can do by our own natural abilities, but the supernatural gift of faith we have received as a gift from God. Our capacity to love God and worship Him is "because God's love has been poured out into our hearts through the Holy Spirit who has been given to us" (Rom 5:5). Through this faith that comes to us from God, He has adopted us as His sons and daughters in Christ. It is this divine filiation that is the deepest source of our identity and the bond that unites us as the ecclesial family.

*How we pray is then intimately connected with how we believe and understand ourselves as Christians and our relationship to Christ?*

The ancient Latin axiom "lex orandi, lex credendi" expresses this truth—the law of prayer is the law of belief. In other words, the content and manner of our liturgical worship deeply form our understanding and approach to our faith in Christ. When this principle is fully embraced and lived out, our prayer becomes the purest expression of our belief, and our belief in turn animates and directs our prayer. Worshiping in spirit and truth, we allow the sacred mysteries gradually to refashion us according to the pattern of Christ, the perfect image of the Father. This is the ultimate goal of our participation in the liturgy—that we might be "conformed to the image of his Son" (Rom 8:29), and so share more fully in the inner life of the Most Holy Trinity, the communion of eternal love.

# Part IV

# The Path of Liturgical Renewal

9

# THE ROLE OF THE CLERGY

PETER CARTER: *Your Eminence, some readers may be familiar with the story of Dom Prosper Guéranger, who worked to restore the Benedictine monastic tradition in nineteenth-century France. With the political upheavals of the French Revolution, monastic life in France had been legally abolished, and monasteries were disbanded. Dom Guéranger stands out as a pioneer of his time, reestablishing the monastery at Solesmes in 1833, only the second monastery in France to be reestablished following the French Revolution.*

*Today, we find ourselves roughly fifty years after the Second Vatican Council. Some have compared Vatican II to the French Revolution, with Cardinal Suenens quoted as saying, "Vatican II is the French Revolution in the Church."*[1] *In the years following Vatican II, much of the Church's liturgical, musical, and artistic tradition was either neglected or lost, with many new initiatives of restoration and renewal only now beginning to take root. In the desperate situation that the Church finds herself in today, what lessons might we learn from Dom Guéranger, especially in regard to the preservation and renewal of the Church's traditions?*

ROBERT CARDINAL SARAH: Dom Guéranger suffered greatly. He was a man of immense courage, persevering in the face of countless difficulties. What we need today is that same faith, indefectible courage, and perseverance. We must be

[1] Quoted in Archbishop Marcel Lefebvre, *An Open Letter to Confused Catholics*, trans. Father M. Crowdy (Fowler Wright Books for the Society of St. Pius X, 1986), 105.

men and women of deep faith, truly believing that God has called us to dedicate ourselves entirely to Him. We must not be afraid or weary, but have great love of God, fidelity to the Sacred Scriptures, the holy traditions, and the Magisterium. The group of diocesan priests who joined Dom Guéranger had nothing—no living tradition to guide them. They were compelled to rediscover it themselves, as it had ceased to exist. This required great love and humility, to begin again as if from nothing.

We often fixate on numbers to determine the success of our efforts, asking, How many?: How many will join us? How many will be needed to make a difference? Instead, we need to focus on our own response to God's call, praying like Isaiah, "Here am I! Send me" (Is 6:8), and firmly cling to Jesus Christ's love: "Who shall separate us from the love of Christ? Shall tribulation, or distress, or persecution, or famine, or nakedness, or peril, or sword? As it is written, 'For your sake we are being killed all day long; we are regarded as sheep to be slaughtered.' No, in all these things we are more than conquerors through him who loved us" (Rom 8:35–37).

*Yes, this focus on numbers certainly reflects a human, sociological attitude. It even reminds me that the Jews in Jesus' time wanted a Messiah who would overthrow their Roman oppressors, not a savior who would say, "Take up your cross and follow me" (see Mt 16:24). The same seems true today.*

And we must remember that Christ started with just twelve, calling them one by one. The success of any renewal depends not on the multitudes, but on the faithfulness of the few. And today, rather than just the first twelve, we have more than five thousand, five hundred bishops in the world and more than four hundred thousand priests.

What's most informative and revealing about the example of the monks of Solesmes is that they did not take the rupture with continuity as an opportunity to reinvent the Church or her tradition of sacred music. Instead, after founding their community, their top priority was to reestablish tradition—first, in following the original Rule of Saint Benedict as it had been written more than twelve hundred years earlier, and then in their approach to the liturgy and liturgical music, as they began gathering ancient manuscripts of Gregorian chant throughout Europe. It is vital not to cut ourselves off from our roots, our Sacred Tradition, and our very ancient heritage.

*There is a common joke that for any problem a person might have, "There is an app for that." However, the facetious phrase seems to reflect a real attitude in the Church today that we need new and novel solutions to the Church's problem—new structures, new organizations, even new forms of the liturgy, as if the latest novelty will finally realize Christ's vision of salvation for the world. But, as you have noted in writings before, it is not a restructuring of the Roman Curia that will finally solve the Church's problems, nor will any new program or initiative on its own merits.*

We don't need a new sacrament to finally realize the vision of holiness—the call and the means to holiness has not changed and remains accessible to all who "have ears to hear". What we must do to become holy is clear: We need simply to convert ourselves deeply to the Gospel of Jesus Christ, to imitate Christ's way of living, to be confirmed in that path, and to pursue holiness with diligence and patience. Otherwise, the process of change and the allure of novelty risks becoming an end in itself. We begin to think that in the liturgy we must always be actively doing something, introducing, inventing or changing something rather than pausing to ask whether the liturgy is changing us. Are we truly lifting our hearts and minds to God? Do we really believe in God and love Him with all our heart, with all our soul, and with all our strength? Do we truly believe in the power and holiness of the sacraments? These are the questions that we should be asking ourselves.

Reform, whether liturgically or structurally, is often misunderstood as change for its own sake. But theologically, reform means returning to the sources, getting back onto the right path. Reform is certainly necessary, but we need not invent a new way of being the Church. At best, this becomes a distraction—a waste of time, money, and energy. At worst, it can devolve into an ideological revolution. The only thing that Christ is asking of us is conversion and repentance: "The time is fulfilled, and the kingdom of God is at hand; repent, and believe in the gospel" (Mk 1:15). To promote a revolution against the truths of the Church would be to revolt against Christ, who is the Truth! The Second Vatican Council is properly understood only in terms of its call and potential for a reform of the Church, not a revolution of the Church that undermines its essence.

## *The Politicization of Latin*

*After the publication of the Novus Ordo Missae in 1969, it seems that Pope Paul VI sought a genuine reform of post-conciliar sacred music—not a revolution—in the 1974 letter* Voluntati obsequens *and the* Jubilate Deo *chants, which contained the "bare minimum repertoire" of Gregorian chant for the whole Church. Nevertheless, there is sometimes a reluctance or fear among some priests and musicians in restoring the use of Latin in the liturgy, even in using the simple* Jubilate Deo *chants. This apprehension appears to stem from concerns about being a liturgical outlier in one's diocese or be-*

*ing written off as a "traditionalist" or a supposed opponent of Pope Francis. I find this misunderstanding laughable since it is so far removed from reality: Not only did Vatican II call for Latin to be retained in the liturgy, but the very Masses that Pope Francis celebrates today regularly include Latin and Gregorian chant. What do you think is the root cause of this resistance toward the use of Latin in the liturgy?*

The aversion to Latin and Gregorian chant is rooted in an ideology of liturgical revolution that asserts that the Church's identity has changed. Again, Pope Benedict's words regarding the pre-conciliar liturgical books that I have already mentioned are also true in regard to Latin: "What earlier generations held as sacred, remains sacred and great for us too, and it cannot be all of a sudden entirely forbidden or even considered harmful."[2] To promote revolution is to echo the words of Lucifer, the first revolutionary, when he said, "I will not serve."

To restore the use of Latin in the liturgy, we are also faced with the reality that many priests and bishops today remain ignorant of the Church's liturgical and theological traditions, and this lack of knowledge makes it challenging for them to grasp their importance. The failure of many seminaries to provide a foundational education in Latin makes this connection challenging but not impossible. Our formation is never finished, even when we are ordained priests! We must recognize that we are linked with the saints, the Fathers of the Church, and the Apostles—with the prayer of the Church throughout the ages! We must recognize and affirm our tradition because it will make us grow in our faith and in love of Christ and His Church. It is truly naivety and arrogance to sever oneself from tradition, and this only results in spiritual impoverishment.

[2] Benedict XVI, motu proprio *Summorum pontificum* (July 7, 2007).

There is also a risk for a priest today of becoming a liturgical innovator, a showman where he is the star. If he must decide for himself how to celebrate the Mass for his community, not drawing from tradition, then he risks putting aside his priesthood to become an entertainer in a church based on his own cult of personality. We could almost call it a form of subjectivism—a tendency to rely on one's own feelings, rather than receiving from the wisdom of tradition. But when we speak of faith, I must receive everything from God, from the saints, and from the Apostles, like a child. My task is not to create, but simply to receive what has been handed down, and then to pass on what I have received, without creating it anew myself. Christ is the one who makes "all things new" (Rev 21:5). How urgent it is to take seriously the words we daily repeat during the Holy Mass and to learn to say humbly, like Saint Paul: "For I received from the Lord what I also delivered to you, that the Lord Jesus on the night when he was betrayed took bread, and when he had given thanks, he broke it, and said: 'This is my body which is for you. Do this in remembrance of me.'" (1 Cor 11:23–24).

*Many laymen—and perhaps even some priests—may be unaware that the tombs of Saints Peter and Paul are in Rome, along with those of other biblical figures and numerous martyrs of the early Church. There is something powerful about being in those sacred spaces, standing on the same ground where they stood. Upon visiting Rome, one's understanding of one's Christian identity deepens, as the successor of Saint Peter stands above his tomb, continuing his ministry today. Even the connection to the Latin language becomes clearer when acknowledging the historical reality that most Catholics belong to the Latin Rite, the Roman Church founded by Saint Peter.*

A priest without roots, who is unaware of this heritage, would be like Saint Paul if he tried to follow Christ alone, without the other Apostles. Just as Paul had to meet the Apostles and learn the tradition from them, so we must be connected to the Church's tradition. Even when Paul was converted on the road to Damascus, it was tradition, in the person of Ananias, that guided him. Paul could not teach himself and be a Christian in isolation, even though he had received a solid education in the law from a famous and well-respected Rabbi, Gamaliel. He had to be linked with Ananias, who was certainly less educated in the Scriptures, so that he could lead him in the fullness of the mystery of Jesus Christ. We all have to learn from our Ananiases.

It is a crisis when priests innovate on their own, without knowledge of or reference to tradition. Growth cannot occur in isolation; a tree must have roots if it is to bear fruit. Just as Saint Jerome said that "ignorance of the Scriptures is ignorance of Christ",[3] so also is ignorance of tradition an ignorance of Christ and His Church. Therefore, it is vital to train priests with at least a rudimentary knowledge of Latin so that they can celebrate the Mass in the language of the Church. Even my own father, who knew very little Latin, learned to pray the basic Latin prayers. which helped him to grow in his faith and identity as a Christian.

## *Pursuing Liturgical Renewal*

*What advice would you give to a priest starting out as a new pastor regarding the liturgy and the sacred music in his parish? What should his priorities be?*

[3] Saint Jerome, *The First Book of the Commentary on Isaiah*, in *St. Jerome: Commentary on Isaiah*, trans. Thomas P. Scheck, Ancient Christian Writers 68 (Newman Press, 2015), no. 1.

I would begin by emphasizing formation, especially biblical formation. It is essential to help the faithful understand the profound meaning of what we celebrate in the liturgy. The center of our life is Christ, and our liturgical celebrations of Christ's life, death, and Resurrection must be done properly, with reverence and beauty. This is particularly vital today when so many have lost belief in the real presence of Christ in the Eucharist. Without Christ as the center of our lives, we are spiritually dead. I would also encourage him to make it a priority to help people enter more deeply into the mystery of their baptism. As Pope Benedict XVI so beautifully expressed, to be baptized is to be immersed into the very life of the Most Holy Trinity.[4] We must reclaim this sense of baptismal identity and vocation.

When it comes to shaping the sacred music of a parish, we are not left to rely solely on our instincts, experiences, and preferences. We have clear criteria laid out by Saint Pius X and affirmed by every pope since him for discerning what musical forms are truly suitable for divine worship. As we have discussed, there are three requirements: The music must be sacred, possess goodness of form (usually understood as artistic integrity and beauty), and have a sense of universality. Amidst the vast array of musical styles, we can recognize that which can properly be called "sacred music"—music that reflects the attributes of God and that is directed as an offering of praise to God and for the sanctification of the faithful.

*What would your advice be to priests who find themselves lacking in liturgical and musical formation, but who desire to learn and grow in these areas now?*

[4] Benedict XVI, Angelus, Feast of the Baptism of the Lord (Saint Peter's Square, January 8, 2006).

Regrettably, for many priests today, their most formative liturgical experiences were in seminaries where the music was far removed from the richness of the Church's tradition of sacred music. This crisis of inadequate formation gravely affects the priesthood and then extends beyond the priests to the laity. In many places, we have lost a genuine understanding of the very essence of the liturgy, the nature of the priesthood, and its sacred purpose. Priests who find themselves in a situation of having received poor formation must cultivate great humility and patience so that they can be continually formed in the true nature of the liturgy.

For this reason, it is crucial that every priest receive thorough formation in his sacred office as a minister of almighty God. This formation cannot merely be academic study, but must encompass the riches of the Church's artistic and liturgical traditions, present in centuries past and still alive today. Rather than hastily embracing novelties or focusing solely on external matters, we must recognize that our entire lives are meant to be an act of worship and praise to God. This requires profound interior conversion, shaping us to pray truly with sincerity from the heart, with bodies and souls united in offering fitting adoration. It is not enough simply to teach the tenets of the faith. We must allow Christ to transform us so that our very being bears witness to unwavering faith and trust in Him, even amidst suffering and adversity. To achieve this kind of radical configuration to Christ the High Priest, priests must themselves continually pursue ongoing formation and grow spiritually through retreats.

When we find our formation lacking, we must turn to our Lord in humble prayer, trusting that He will guide His Church in making our worship ever more transcendent and radiant with His divine beauty. The disciples themselves implored our Lord, "Teach us to pray" (Lk 11:1). Authentic prayer is not mere recitation of the sacred texts, but a "putting on of Christ" (see Rom 13:14), which renews us and leads us to true holiness of life. The renewal of sacred liturgy is then an ongoing process that we must renew in ourselves in every encounter with Christ. I especially recommend for priests to take their retreats at monasteries so that they can immerse themselves in the full and authentic liturgical life of the Church chanted in the Divine Office and the conventual Mass. The complete dedication to a life of prayer as expressed in the monastic tradition has always been a source of spiritual renewal for individual priests and for the whole Church.

I would also encourage priests to approach the challenges they face as opportunities to imitate Christ by embracing the cross. Just as our Lord faced opposition and misunderstanding, even from religious authorities, priests today must be prepared to encounter resistance and discouragement in their efforts to renew the liturgy and sacred music in their parishes. However, this should not dampen their zeal or creativity. Like Dom Guéranger and the monks of Solesmes, who persevered in the face of immense challenges to restore the Benedictine tradition and Gregorian chant, priests must be resourceful in finding ways to deepen their own liturgical formation and to share the riches of the Church's liturgical heritage with their people. The success of any efforts to renew the liturgy and sacred music in our parishes and dioceses will depend not on our own strength or cleverness, but on our openness to the transformative power of God's grace. As Christ Himself teaches us, if we "seek first his kingdom and his righteousness" (Mt 6:33), all the rest will be provided for us. This is the lesson that Dom Guéranger and his monks learned through their daily fidelity to prayer and the liturgy, even in the face of opposition and hardship. It is a lesson that we too must take to heart as we strive to renew and elevate the worship of the Church in our own time. We should not be swayed by the changing winds of popular opinion or the pressure to conform to cultural norms. Instead, we should have the courage to be countercultural, to stake everything on our Lord and His promises. If we lead by example, if we truly "put out into the deep" (Lk 5:4) and trust in the Lord's guidance, I am convinced that a new springtime of liturgical renewal will blossom in ways we cannot yet imagine. But it begins with our own *fiat*, our own "let it be to me according to your word" (Lk 1:38), our own willingness to surrender ourselves to Christ, especially through our encounter with Him in the liturgy.

Great consolation can always be found in participating in the liturgies of certain churches, cathedrals, and monasteries, where fidelity to liturgical norms and tradition have taken root and born abundant fruit. The heavenly chanting of monasteries is renowned, and whenever we encounter the liturgy celebrated in an exemplary way, we cannot help but be inspired by the awesome beauty of God present in the Church's liturgy.

*Unfortunately, in many places, liturgies that are truly reverent and beautiful are rare, especially when combined with excellent music programs. Why do you think this is the case, and what can be done to address it?*

The scarcity of truly beautiful and reverent liturgical celebrations in many parts of the Church today is a tragic situation, but it is not due to a lack of noble efforts. There are several reasons for this: Firstly, the widespread lack of faith and the eclipse of God and consequently the loss of the sense of the sacred in our secularized society has seeped into the Church herself. When the transcendent and divine nature of the liturgy is no longer understood or appreciated, it becomes easy to settle for mediocrity or even banality in our worship.

Secondly, there is sometimes resistance and even opposition to efforts to promote liturgical beauty and reverence from clergy and ecclesiastical authorities who, at times, seem to have lost sight of the true nature and purpose of the sacred liturgy. This can be discouraging for those working to renew and elevate our liturgical celebrations, but we must look to the examples of the reforming saints, who always faced obstacles from within the Church herself.

Where liturgies are celebrated with great beauty and reverence and with care for the sacred music, it is often the result of the courageous and countercultural work of dedicated priests and faithful and true artists—musicians and artisans who devotedly offer their talents and their very lives with great generosity, sometimes laboring for years under difficult circumstances and with little support. The Church owes these individuals a debt of gratitude commensurate with their selfless dedication.

*The building up of a culture of beauty and the arts takes generations—starting one school, training one musician at a time. There is often a lack of financial resources to build these institutions, and the process can take decades before having a widespread impact. How should Catholics, whether clergy or laity, go about trying to renew the Church's liturgical culture, especially when achieving a widespread renewal in our lifetimes is often dismissed as wishful thinking?*

To address this situation, we must all work to restore a deep sense of the sacred and an understanding of the true nature and purpose of the liturgy, among both the clergy and the faithful. We must also support and encourage those who are already working to promote liturgical beauty and reverence, whether they are artists, musicians, or simply faithful Catholics who deeply love the Church and her liturgical tradition. This support should come from all levels of the Church, from the hierarchy to the grassroots, and can take many forms—spiritual, moral, and financial.

It is important to remember that the restoration of Gregorian chant, which the Abbey of Solesmes is known for today, was not fully realized during the lifetime of its founder, Dom Guéranger. Even Moses was never permitted to enter the Promised Land. Similarly, we must not lose hope if we do not see the full fruits of our labors in renewing the Church's liturgical and musical traditions in our own lifetimes. This should not discourage us, but rather, we must trust in God's providence and timing. The seeds we sow today may not bear full fruit for many years to come. But if we remain steadily faithful to the Church's teachings and traditions, if we continue to work tirelessly to build up a culture of beauty and the arts, we can be confident that our efforts will not be in vain. As Saint Paul adjures us, "Let us not grow weary in well-doing, for in due season we shall reap, if we do not lose heart" (Gal 6:9). We must persevere in our efforts, no matter how small or seemingly insignificant they may appear. Every school that is established, every musician that is trained, every work of beauty that is created for the glory of God is a step forward. We must not become discouraged by the magnitude of the task or the difficulties and resistance that we face. The Church's missionary identity has always been one of transformation through personal encounter, one person at a time. Just as Christ chose twelve men to be His Apostles and to spread the Gospel to the ends of the earth, we too must focus on forming and supporting those individuals who will be the leaven in the dough, the salt of the earth, and the light of the world (see Mt 5:13–14). By investing in these individuals and communities, and by persevering in our own efforts to live and worship in a manner worthy of our calling, we can trust that God will bring about the renewal of the Church's liturgical life in His own time and way.

*What role do you see for bishops in leading the renewal of the liturgy and sacred music in their dioceses? What would you say to bishops who may be hesitant to initiate efforts toward renewal or resistant to doing so, perhaps out of fear of "sticking out" and being judged by either the media or their brother bishops?*

I would humbly try to explain and make known to them that, as a pastor, every bishop must remember that he is not exercising his own personal and human authority but is acting "in persona Christi". He is not to impose his personal preferences, his own opinions on liturgy. He must endeavor to transmit and hand on the sacred heritage of the Church. He must act like Jesus did and hand on what He Himself has received from the Father. "No longer do I call you servants, for the servant does not know what his master is doing; but I have called you friends, for all that I have heard from my Father I have made known to you" (Jn 15:15). The bishop must say like Saint Paul: "For I received from the Lord what I also delivered to you, that the Lord Jesus on the night he was betrayed took bread" (1 Cor 11:23). Each bishop must be aware of this: "The pope's authority"—and obviously that of the bishop and the priest—"is bound to the Tradition of faith, and that also applies to the liturgy. It is not 'manufactured' by the authorities. Even the pope can only be a humble servant of its lawful development and abiding integrity and identity."[5] What we must all understand is this: The liturgy is above all God's gift of worship to the

[5] Joseph Cardinal Ratzinger, *The Spirit of the Liturgy* (Ignatius Press, 2000), 166.

Church. "The Liturgy derives its greatness from what it is, not from what we do with it. . . . Liturgy is not an expression of the community's consciousness, which in any case is diffuse and changing. It is revelation received in faith and prayer."[6]

As the chief liturgists of their dioceses, bishops have a crucial role in influencing a larger number of people through their actions, especially in their own dioceses but even beyond. They should not be afraid to be at the forefront of this renewal, leading by example. The liturgical celebrations of the cathedral should be the model for all parishes in the diocese, and the example of how reverence, beauty, and sacred music can be worthily celebrated in fidelity to the Church's norms.

To my brother bishops who may be hesitant, I would say this: Do not be afraid to embrace the Church's rich liturgical and musical heritage, for it is a matter of fidelity to the Lord and to His Bride, the Church! It is not a matter of personal preference or nostalgia. The Second Vatican Council called for a renewed appreciation and a "careful investigation" of the Church's venerable liturgical traditions, not a rupture with the past.[7]

*What about situations where faithful Catholics, especially musicians, want to serve the Church and help renew the liturgy, but feel discouraged by their pastor or their bishop? What can be done, especially for the young people who feel called to serve the Church in this way but are sometimes turned away or labeled too traditional or conservative?*

I would say to these pastors, bishops, and lay faithful: Do not act for your own glory or the glory of your own name or

[6] Joseph Ratzinger, "The Theology of the Liturgy," in *Theology of the Liturgy*, trans. John Saward et al. (Ignatius Press, 2014), 557.

[7] Vatican Council II, Constitution on the Sacred Liturgy *Sacrosanctum concilium* (December 4, 1963), no. 23.

reputation in serving the Church, but for the glorification of God and the salvation of souls. To those who want to serve but who are discouraged, do not give up! Continue to pray, study, and deepen your knowledge and love for the Church and her traditions. Explore possibilities such as nearby monasteries that may welcome your desire to learn and serve the Church. Seek out communities of support and mutual encouragement while always being faithful to the Church. For young people without support, this can lead to lost vocations—a tragic situation and a grave responsibility for pastors and bishops who fail to recognize and foster these vocations. If any of you feel abandoned, you must not give up hope! You must imitate Christ who was not afraid to give His life for the Church despite His disciples' abandonment of Him in the Garden of Gethsemane.

Bishops and priests have a grave responsibility to imitate Christ, who always sought to gather people to Himself and involve them in His saving work. If they fail to do this, it can be deeply discouraging, but despite these challenges, we must persevere. I am reminded of a young man I met in Ars who came from Belgium with a desire to enter monastic life, but not in his own country. His bishop had told him there would be no singing of the Divine Office, and no opportunity for the traditional forms of the liturgy. This is a great tragedy! These are indeed difficult times, but also times of great grace, for they are Christ's. We must follow His example of humble perseverance when we are faced with misunderstanding and opposition.

10

# THE RESTORATION OF THE DIVINE OFFICE

PETER CARTER: *You mentioned to me that witnessing the priests of your parish praying was one of the most formative experiences of your childhood. Can you elaborate on that and how it shaped your own vocation to the priesthood?*

ROBERT CARDINAL SARAH: Indeed, observing the priests in prayer at various times throughout the day had a profound impact on me as a child. Seeing them gather in the church every morning and midday, I came to understand that they must be encountering *someone*, someone great, important, and vital for their life and ministry. This realization inspired me and sparked within me a deep desire to serve God through a life of prayer. Speaking from my own experience, I believe that it is crucial for the faithful, and especially children, to witness their priests engaged in prayer. This powerful testimony communicates that priests are, first and foremost, men of prayer. It is through prayer that we become holy, directing our entire being toward God to become like Him. Christ Himself declared, "Apart from me you can do nothing" (Jn 15:5). Prayer, then, is indispensable for a priest, both for his own sanctification and for the fulfillment of his pastoral duties. We are called not to a life of isolation, but rather to be living witnesses to the truth that the Church is indeed the dwelling place of God on earth. In order to lead others to Christ, we must first seek and encounter Him ourselves in prayer and in contemplation of the Word of God.

We need only look to the example of Saint John Vianney, the Curé of Ars, who transformed an entire village through his ceaseless prayer. The profound words of Dom Jean-Baptiste Chautard ring true: "If the priest is a saint . . . the people will be fervent; if the priest is fervent, the people will be pious; if the priest is pious, the people will at least be decent. But if the priest is only decent, the people will be godless. The spiritual generation is always one degree less intense in its life than the one who beget it in Christ."[1] To lead others to God effectively, one must first personally encounter Him and have a relationship with Him.

It is not through structural changes or reforms that we progress in holiness. Holiness is achieved as we change and reform ourselves through our encounter with God each day in prayer. Consider Christ who, for thirty years in Nazareth, led a life centered on prayer and work, remaining silent. And before commencing His public ministry, He spent forty days and forty nights in solitude, praying, and fasting. It is therefore crucial for priests to be men of prayer, not only for their own sanctification but also as a way of leading the laity as a faithful witness, especially for the young who are discerning their own vocations.

## *The Divine Office as Communal Prayer*

*The Second Vatican Council strongly encourages clerics to pray the Divine Office in common, even urging them to sing it when possible: "Since the Divine Office is the voice of the Church, that is of the whole mystical body publicly praising God, those clerics who are*

[1] Jean-Baptiste Chautard, *Soul of the Apostolate* (TAN Books, 2008), 40–41.

*not obliged to office in choir, especially priests who live together or who assemble for any purpose, are urged to pray at least some part of the divine office in common. . . . It is, moreover, fitting that the office, both in choir and in common, be sung when possible."*[2] *However, the lived experience of many priests in parishes today is that the Divine Office is often prayed alone and in private, as if it were a personal devotion. And even when it is prayed in common, it is often recited with little or no singing. It seems that in practice, the Church has generally lost the understanding that the Divine Office is, of its very nature, meant to be prayed in community and sung. What would you say to those who desire to implement the Church's vision of praying and singing the Divine Office in common, but who may fear that such a practice would be foreign or unrealistic outside of a seminary or monastic setting?*

The reality of ecclesial life today is complex and difficult because Western society acts and lives in silent apostasy, as if God were dead. A deep crisis of faith and vocations is causing seminaries to close in Europe and is overworking many priests, who move from parish to parish, which wears them out spiritually, physically, and psychologically and reduces or removes their time for prayer and silent adoration before the Blessed Sacrament. Churches are being closed, sold, and in some cases, demolished or desecrated. The number of practicing faithful in most Western countries is decreasing, and participation in Sunday Mass seems optional. In this scenario, the priority for lay people necessarily revolves around the celebration of the Sunday Eucharist, but secondarily around the celebration of the Divine Office and other religious devotions.

[2] Vatican Council II, Constitution on the Sacred Liturgy *Sacrosanctum concilium* (December 4, 1963), no. 99.

The text you quoted from *Sacrosanctum concilium* beautifully articulates the importance of the Divine Office, especially when communally celebrated in song. In fact, the Office is essentially a sung contemplation of God through the praying of the sacred texts from both Divine revelation and the tradition of the Church. The clergy have the obligation to recite the entire Divine Office daily, although there is great freedom in the manner in which this is done so that the priests might fulfill their other pastoral obligations without hindrance.

After years of confusion and the abandonment of liturgical practices, much of the Church has forgotten how to celebrate the liturgy as fully and beautifully as possible. Sometimes, apart from honorable exceptions, we are no longer able to remember how to celebrate a solemn Vespers or what Lauds in a cathedral looks like, or even a fully sung Mass. Papal celebrations seem to come from a distant world—from a reality to which we may belong but that is not duplicable, remaining unattainable or even undesirable. In reality, though, we are all called to follow the liturgical rubrics, and to implement fully the Church's liturgical life whether in a small parish or the cathedral of a diocese, each according to his abilities and resources. The Holy Mass is always the same Holy Mass, the liturgy is always the same liturgy. But to the best of our ability, we must celebrate every liturgy with beauty and solemnity because it is God in His majesty whom we adore and worship.

*I hope that we can help inspire a few priests and bishops reading this to take seriously the idea of singing the Divine Office in common in their dioceses. However, I know some priests who are trying to do this but who lack support from other clergy in their diocese or even from their bishops, since they believe that the practice is foreign or in-*

*applicable to diocesan priests and that it is only proper in seminaries or monasteries. Why would it be more beneficial to pray the Divine Office in community rather than to pray it privately?*

There are many reasons one could give for praying in community, but the best reason is also the simplest: because Christ asked us to pray together, as a community of believers: "For where two or three are gathered in my name, there am I in the midst of them" (Mt 18:20). Of course we should always be praying individually, but it takes deliberate effort to pray with others, together as one Church. And whenever we pray this way, we are visibly fulfilling Christ's prayer "that they may all be one" (Jn 17:21).

If priests regularly pray the Divine Office privately, they can be tempted to neglect their obligation to pray the Divine Office out of fatigue and the busyness of their pastoral duties. However, if the Divine Office is celebrated by the community, then avoiding the obligation becomes much more difficult, since they are accountable to each other rather than only to themselves. There is a certain discipline that is required whenever we pray with others, a certain giving up of our own will and personal comfort. This is the type of discipline that is especially needed for priests and bishops to lead their flock effectively. At times, it may feel like a joy, and at other times like a cross, but if it ever feels like a cross, it must be embraced daily with love, for from it flows the grace of Christ.

Even if a priest is alone in a parish, he could sometimes invite the faithful to join him in the church at a fixed time to pray morning or evening prayer. In some parishes, priests celebrate Morning Prayer before the morning Mass, and provide booklets for the faithful to join in. And even if the priest is not always present, the people can still pray Morning

Prayer in the church on their own, though ideally it is the priest who should lead them in this. And when the priest prays the Divine Office alone, he can still go to the church, giving public witness to his fidelity to praying all of the liturgical hours of the Church. I want to emphasize going into the church to pray, making time in our schedule to speak with God.

The priest must be holy! He must be a man of prayer! God is encountered more easily in the church than in meetings. When a priest looks at his schedule, there should be more meetings with God than with people, as Christ had to leave the crowd to speak to the Father. Moses left the Israelites to speak with God on Mount Sinai. Also Elijah. Like them, we must leave our crowds and go to encounter God in His holy temple. There is comfort and safety in staying with the crowd rather than departing to encounter God in solitude, which can feel unnecessary or inconvenient. Leaving our comfort zones to enter God's house to pray requires effort and humility.

*In terms of organizing liturgical celebrations of Lauds, Vespers, or Compline, it seems that trying to gauge their success only in terms of numbers of attendees goes back to the misguided, sociological mindset we discussed before that thinks only in terms of measurable data. However, even if the priest prays alone, like Moses on Mount Sinai, this act of radical fidelity seems immensely beneficial both for him and for the whole Church. What words of encouragement would you offer to all those seeking to restore the praying of the Divine Office in common?*

Given the current hardships facing the Church, promoting a communal sung celebration of the Divine Office may appear difficult or even daring. For those who have courageously begun this renewal already, I commend them and encourage them to continue with diligence and perseverance. When done with great love and patience, these initiatives will certainly bear abundant fruit. It is not for us to ask when we might see the full restoration and flowering of the liturgical practice of the Church, the "Kingdom of Israel", but to listen faithfully to Christ's words that "It is not for you to know times or seasons which the Father has fixed by his own authority. But you shall receive power when the Holy Spirit has come upon you; and you shall be my witnesses in Jerusalem and in all Judea and Samaria and to the end of the earth" (Acts 1:7–8).

The success of liturgical prayer is measured not by numbers but by faithfulness and great love in our hearts. As Mother Teresa is known for saying: In this life we cannot do great things. We can only do small things with great love. Where the priest celebrates the Divine Office publicly in church, regardless of how many join him, his witness allows people gradually to understand and embrace this source of immense grace. In this sense, we need leaders unafraid to lead by example, celebrating the full liturgy fervently even if alone.

In my native Guinea, where 75 percent of the population is Muslim, the Muslim faithful pray five times daily without fail. We as Catholics are called to render praise to God seven times per day, as the Psalmist declares: "Seven times a day I praise you for your righteous ordinances" (Ps 119:164). The Church prays these words in the Divine Office, but if we are not indeed praying seven times a day, then we are lying to God! We must take seriously the praying of the full Divine Office as our daily prayer, united with the Church throughout the world. Is that too much to consecrate to our loving Father half an hour more to pray Terce, Sext, and None? Jesus and the Apostles "were going up to the temple at the hour of prayer, the ninth hour" (Acts 3:1). "Peter went up on the housetop to pray, about the sixth hour" (Acts 10:9). "Four days ago, about this hour, I was keeping the ninth hour of prayer in my house" (Acts 10:30).

Saint Benedict, the father of Western monasticism, articulated in his Rule a model of coming together for liturgical prayer that the clergy today, both religious and secular, can learn and benefit from in their own liturgical celebrations. We priests must support and encourage one another in this spiritual practice of coming together as brothers to sing the praises of God and to learn in the school of prayer. There is a certain asceticism in singing together that is purifying to the soul and that helps us lead each other in charity through the narrow gate that leads to eternal life (see Mt 7:14).

*In the choir rehearsals at my parish, I often speak about the chants and psalms that we sing as encompassing the full spectrum of human emotions—not just the joyful ones, but also the ones of sorrow, anger, and brokenness, begging for God's mercy and for a fulfillment of His promises. I always find it so human and encouraging that the psalms elevate all of the human emotion and feelings we experience throughout our lives and direct them toward God, transforming them into prayer.*

The psalms often present joy, praise, and thanks, but also grave suffering and feelings of despondency. "Out of the depths I cry to you, O Lord" (Psalm 130:1). But through singing the psalms as an act of praise, our suffering is offered to God, who always looks upon us as a loving Father. The depth of the Scriptures and the liturgy is there to call us back, to return to again and again. Their origin is truly divine and given to us as a gift from God, and so we must be constant in returning to them, since through them we grow to see and understand God more deeply, and consequently to see and understand ourselves and our own lives through God's eyes.

## *The Role of the Bishop*

*What do you think are some practical steps that bishops could take in their dioceses to instruct both their priests and the faithful on the importance of both the Mass and the Divine Office?*

The bishop is called to teach his diocese how to pray, being the first example and witness of liturgical prayer. Bishops must lead by example, teaching their flocks in the school of prayer that is the liturgy of the Church. Just as Jesus often withdrew to pray, the bishop must lead the priests and people of God in prayer, following Christ's example. Throughout salvation history, the Old Testament prophets periodically withdraw from the crowds and into solitude to seek God's guidance through intense prayer. Bishops, too, must be witnessed by the faithful as preeminently men of deep interior prayer, not for an outward show of piety, but as authentic witnesses, examples, and spiritual fathers who lead their flocks in prayer. It is only by first grounding himself in both private and public prayer that the bishop can then fruitfully shepherd his diocese in the Church's communal prayer. He cannot carry the overwhelming weight of his pastoral office by his own strength, but must rely profoundly on God's help obtained through wholehearted prayer, just as Moses did during his solitary vigils. When possible, bishops should make themselves visible and available through the regular celebration of Sunday Mass at their cathedrals, just as pastors should in their parishes. If it is only possible to see the bishop when he is administering the sacrament of confirmation, then he is neglecting a crucial part of his pastoral role. And while social and other pastoral issues are important, the day should begin and end with prayer and teaching his children how to pray. Charity and social justice must flow from a life rooted in prayer. "Seek first his kingdom and his righteousness, and all these things shall be yours as well" (Mt 6:33). Even when it is not possible for him to celebrate the liturgy publicly, bishops must ensure that the cathedral liturgies are celebrated in an exemplary way, showing the way for the rest of the diocese. My friend the late Cardinal Pell exemplified this well by celebrating the main sung Mass at his cathedral every Sunday when he was not obligated to be elsewhere. At Saint Mary's Cathedral in Sydney, he also implemented the Church's desire for the daily celebration of Vespers. I would encourage bishops throughout the world to do the same insofar as they are able. If we believe in the primacy of prayer, then we must let this show forth in our actions.

*How should bishops address the common tendency to prioritize religious devotions over communal liturgical prayer? This is often seen in many parishes in the United States where, outside of the celebration of Mass, there are no celebrations of the Divine Office, although there are frequent celebrations of various religious devotions.*

Priests must help their parishioners understand that, like the early Christians, we are united as one body when we gather to pray the liturgy. While personal devotions are important and have their place, our primary focus as a Church should be on praying the liturgy with one heart and one voice. The celebration of the Eucharist is truly the "fount and apex of the whole Christian life",[3] and when we pray the Mass and

[3] Vatican Council II, Dogmatic Constitution of the Church *Lumen gentium* (November 21, 1964), no. 11.

the Divine Office, we are praying with the whole Church united on earth, in purgatory, and in heaven! Nevertheless, personal and private devotions can greatly benefit the spiritual life of the faithful, helping them to "pray constantly" (1 Thess 5:17) and leading them into a more fruitful celebration of the liturgy. *Sacrosanctum concilium* eloquently speaks of this:

> The spiritual life, however, is not limited solely to participation in the liturgy. The Christian is indeed called to pray with his brethren, but he must also enter into his chamber to pray to the Father, in secret. . . .
>
> Popular devotions of the Christian people are to be highly commended, provided they accord with the laws and norms of the Church, above all when they are ordered by the Apostolic See. . . .
>
> But these devotions should be so drawn up that they harmonize with the liturgical seasons, accord with the sacred liturgy, are in some fashion derived from it, and lead the people to it, since, in fact, the liturgy by its very nature far surpasses any of them.[4]

*What examples could you point to for bishops who want to establish a richer liturgical life in their cathedrals and dioceses?*

I have already mentioned Cardinal Pell, who did excellent work in reforming and promoting the liturgical life in the archdioceses where he served, both Melbourne and Sydney. In Sydney, he did particularly exemplary work with developing the boys' choir at the cathedral and establishing daily sung Vespers, similar to remarkable choral liturgies at Westminster Cathedral in London. These cathedrals demonstrate that the daily choral celebration of liturgical prayer not only is possible but can truly flourish and enrich

[4] *Sacrosanctum concilium*, nos. 12–13.

the whole Church when they are prioritized. Cathedrals are usually located in major cities, inviting people to participate in the Church's liturgy and integrate it into their spiritual lives. The cathedral clergy are not cloistered monks separated from the world—they are ministers called to lead the prayer of the people of God. And their daily celebration of the liturgy teaches the faithful that despite the busyness of the world, the *opus Dei*, the work of God, must never be neglected and seen as secondary to the work of man. The liturgies at cathedrals set the example for the whole diocese, as they are the beating heart of the local church. If led with diligence and patience, the faithful will respond, and these initiatives will bear much fruit. And whenever priests and lay men and women see their bishop prioritizing liturgical prayer, especially through new celebrations of Vespers and other parts of the Divine Office, they should express their support for these efforts and do their best to participate.

## *Being Formed by the Liturgy*

*Since public celebrations of the Divine Office are unfamiliar to many, how should people seek out to be formed by it, whether priests, seminarians, or the laity?*

For priestly formation, the fullest expression of the liturgy possible in seminaries is essential. The days in the seminary are the main source of liturgical formation for many priests, and if this formation is lacking, then that will affect their whole priestly ministry. The issue must be addressed at the source so that it can be an inspiration and model for the liturgy of their parishes. For the laity, since they are not required to recite the full Divine Office, they may pray with simplified editions of the Divine Office, which can prove very beneficial for their spiritual lives. I would recommend that the lay faithful incorporate as much of the Divine Office into their daily prayers as is possible while fulfilling the obligations of their state of life. Praying Lauds in the morning and Vespers and Compline in the evening should be possible for most people. Beginning and ending the day with prayer must be a priority, and the rest of the Divine Office also helps to continue to orient ourselves to God throughout the day—praying without ceasing.

Pastors should help to provide resources for their parishioners to encourage them in this practice, whether the laity pray these parts of the Divine Office in the privacy of their homes or in communal celebrations in the church. While there exist many resources for praying the essential texts of the Divine Office, much work still needs to be done to provide musical resources for singing the Divine Office. I encourage all who are able to help provide these resources for the good of the Church. But regardless of whether the Divine Office is said or sung, it can still be prayed united in heart and voice with the priests in the church or especially on a daily basis in the home, especially as a family. When the communal celebration of the Divine Office has been taken seriously by the Church, it is reflected in the broader culture. Even in the secular culture of Great Britain, the tradition of Anglican choral Evensong (originating from Vespers) is still broadcast on the BBC and informs British identity and culture. In cultures where there has been a long-standing tradition of Vespers, this tradition remains at risk if the Church does not continue to take the liturgy seriously. And in cultures where celebrating the Divine Office is completely foreign, the Church must act with courage and fortitude in establishing the full celebration of the liturgy in her daily life.

*How would you suggest that a bishop or priest begin implementing the celebration of the Divine Office in a cathedral or parish? What would be a good starting point?*

Before beginning a regular celebration of Vespers at a parish, a pastor might begin by celebrating Vespers during Advent and Lent to educate the faithful on the profound beauty and spiritual riches contained within the Divine Office. The seasons of Advent and Lent, and particularly Holy Week, provide an excellent opportunity to introduce the faithful to a richer liturgical life, since during these times, people tend to be more open and receptive to additional spiritual practices and to coming to the church outside of their Sunday obligation. Offering services such as Tenebrae during Holy Week (a combined celebration of Matins and Lauds) or Vespers or Compline during these sacred seasons can be an effective way to introduce these liturgies gradually into the life of the parish. For many cathedrals and parishes, this process will be a rediscovery of the Church's fuller liturgical tradition, which has often been unfortunately limited to the celebration of the Mass. As a consequence of establishing these liturgical practices, the clergy and laity alike will be formed in the Church's "school of prayer" and will make present the Church's living tradition in their own communities. By faithfully practicing this precious tradition of liturgical prayer, we not only nurture and cultivate the spiritual lives of our communities but safeguard these traditions for future generations so that they too can be taught to love and appreciate the prayer of the Church. However, despite my encouragement in reviving the public celebration of the Divine Office, I do not want to downplay the complementary role that popular pious devotions can have in enriching and benefiting spiritual lives of both clergy and laity.

### *The Complementary Role of Religious Devotions*

*How do religious devotions and cultural expressions of faith complement the liturgy and draw people closer to the sacraments? You have mentioned that pilgrimages are an important religious devotion in your home diocese of Conakry.*

Treasured devotions such as the rosary and the Stations of the Cross help sanctify us by inviting us to meditate on the life, death, and Resurrection of our Lord Jesus Christ. These devotions engage our hearts and imaginations, helping us to draw more closely to the realities of our faith and enabling us to participate more fruitfully in the liturgical celebrations. It is a beautiful thing that many Catholics pray the Stations of the Cross every Friday of Lent, drawing close to our Lord through this form of prayer and meditation. Paraliturgical practices such as these can deeply speak to the hearts of the faithful and help them practice and express their faith in meaningful and tangible ways. However, while these popular devotions and culturally rooted expressions of faith certainly have value, it is crucial to maintain a clear distinction between them and the sacred liturgy itself.

Conflating devotion and localized religious practices with the liturgy or blending them into it can risk undermining the nature and objective importance of the Church's worship, which transcends distinctive cultural expressions and unites the faithful throughout the world. In some parts of Africa, the incorporation of dance, music, and cultural presentations within the Mass itself has become problematic, sometimes extending services excessively to six hours or more! This is a liturgical abuse! The liturgy, that holy communion with God, should remain distinct from the legitimate cultural celebrations that may appropriately precede or follow it. While local traditions can evolve outside the liturgy, the divine liturgy itself must remain inculturated yet immutable, reflecting God's own unchanging nature.

In Guinea, we have a rich tradition of taking pilgrimages to sites of national religious significance, such as the tomb of the catechist Gubuu Yaza, who was martyred in 1927, or to the spot where the Christian missionaries first arrived in Guinea. These pilgrimages provide wonderful opportunities for encountering Christ through prayer, confession, daily Mass, and beautiful processions. I vividly remember the centenary celebration of the mission in Conakry in 1977, where we spent three days on pilgrimage, walking from our parishes. People came from all over to be a part of this pilgrimage, some journeying hundreds of kilometers. We gathered for Morning Prayer on Thursday, and the pilgrimage continued through to Sunday, culminating with Mass. Throughout the several days of pilgrimage, the time is filled not only with walking but with constant prayer, singing, confession, penances, and acts of reparation, and is all centered around the daily celebration of the Mass.

11

# FORMING VOCATIONS OF SERVICE

PETER CARTER: *Your Eminence, if we aim to address liturgical renewal at its root, it seems we must study the preconditions for forming both holy priests and church musicians who, by God's grace, will bring about this renewal to full fruition in the Church. Could you speak about your own experience of discovering your vocation?*

ROBERT CARDINAL SARAH: My vocation to the priesthood began from the witness of faith I encountered in my family, especially through observing my father's devotion to prayer. Seeing him kneel in prayer when he heard the Angelus bell touched me deeply and instilled in me a love for our Lady. My father's example planted the first seeds of my vocation. A pivotal moment occurred when a priest from my parish asked if I had considered entering the seminary. Until then, I had never imagined that an African could become a priest, since all the priests we knew were European. Even my mother thought it impossible. This experience taught me the importance of openly suggesting and encouraging others to consider serving the Lord in this way. Similarly, we must not hesitate to propose the path of priesthood or religious life to others, as God's call is open to everyone. If children witness our dedication to God, they will believe that such a life is possible for them too.

In addition to the primary vocations of priesthood, religious life, and marriage, there is also the calling to use our gifts and talents for the good of the Church and of society.

This is especially important in relation to sacred music. The parable of the talents reminds us to multiply the gifts God has given us, not to hide them away. We are called to share the treasures we have received, not bury them.

Your work, Peter, in training church musicians and introducing young people to the richness of sacred music tradition is a vital ministry. By giving them the education and tools they need to enhance liturgical music in their parishes, you are helping them discover and embrace their own musical vocation. The fact that there have been conversions in your choir, and that some of your choir members have gone on to become music directors themselves, is a testament to the fruitfulness of your efforts and the power of a vocation lived out in service to the Church. I encourage all church musicians to serve the Church with the same love and fidelity that Christ had when He laid down His life out of love for her. "If we have died with Christ, we believe that we shall also live with him" (Rom 6:8).

## *The Family: The First School of Love and Beauty*

*As we have seen with your experience of witnessing your father and parish priests at prayer, early childhood experiences play a crucial role in shaping the hearts and consciences of the next generation. Can you speak to the responsibility of parents in forming the culture of the home? How might they inculcate in their children a love for God, and for beauty and music?*

The family is the first school of love where children initially learn about faith, often through the example of their parents and grandparents.[1] It is within the family that the seeds of

[1] See John Paul II, apostolic exhortation *Familiaris consortio* (On the Role of the Christian Family in the Modern World) (November 22, 1981), nos. 35–37.

love for God are planted. In a father's love, we see a reflection of God the Father's greatness, tenderness, and generosity. From this, a love for art and beauty naturally arises, as everything good comes from God and reflects Him. Children can encounter the beauty and sacredness of God through their experience of the sacred liturgy. Frequent participation in the liturgy, and especially the grand celebrations and solemnities of Christmas and Easter, form the hearts and minds of both children and adults. The liturgy's intrinsic beauty forms and transforms us, serving as the origin of the various ministries and charisms in the Church.

In our modern technological age, parents have an unparalleled opportunity to expose their children to a wide repertoire of sacred music. Access to music from every era and genre has never been easier, allowing people to easily familiarize themselves with the masterworks of sacred music. But with this opportunity also comes the responsibility for parents to guide their children in discovering and appreciating the beauty of sacred music, nurturing a lifelong love for the Church's musical treasures.

*Vatican II states, "The treasure of sacred music is to be preserved and fostered with great care" and "Great importance is to be attached to the teaching and practice of music in seminaries, in the novitiates and houses of study of religious of both sexes, and also in other Catholic institutions and schools. To impart this instruction, teachers are to be carefully trained and put in charge of the teaching of sacred music. It is desirable also to found higher institutes of sacred music whenever this can be done."*[2] *In recent years, many initiatives promoting sacred music have been established, often by lay Catholics who have a love for sacred music and who desire to renew the culture of sacred music in the Church. What words of encouragement would you give*

[2] Vatican Council II, Constitution on the Sacred Liturgy *Sacrosanctum concilium* (December 4, 1963), nos. 114–15.

*to all those, laity or clergy, doing what they can to scatter the seeds of sacred music in their parishes and communities?*

In many countries, courageous men and women of faith and great love for God have taken it upon themselves to introduce music initiatives into their local churches and dioceses. These individuals, some of whom come from professional backgrounds in music, bring a level of expertise and seriousness to their work that has brought hope and renewal to the musical life of their communities, which have frequently suffered from a grave lack of artistic integrity. The tireless work of these artists and musicians has already borne much fruit, for which we give thanks to God. The glorious strains of Gregorian chant have begun once again to resound in many of our churches and parishes, and in many countries, the repertoire of sacred music is being enriched with modern compositions of exceptional quality and beauty. These new compositions must be recognized as legitimate fruits of the Spirit and celebrated and sung alongside the most ancient music from the Church's tradition. What a joy it is to witness the faithful gathered together, singing the Latin chants of the Mass! And whenever the beautiful Latin chants of the Mass and the Marian and Eucharistic hymns are sung, they are given a new voice and made anew in the hearts of the faithful. These efforts to revive and renew the Church's musical patrimony bring hope for the future of sacred music.

However, the struggle against mediocrity and indifference toward the liturgy and sacred music can often lead to discouragement and disappointment if we are too focused on measuring and quantifying success. Like the sower in the parable, we must scatter the seed wherever we can, and the seed sown in fertile ground will yield one hundredfold. As people of faith, we must examine our present circumstances with humility and act in accordance with the teachings of the Church, always working toward a future that is hopeful and filled with promise.

One of the most pressing challenges we face in bringing about a modern renaissance of sacred music is that many of the institutions for young musicians to receive the most thorough musical training are secular institutions that do not support the faith and mission of the Church. The Church today needs new centers of musical and liturgical formation that not only immerse students in the liturgical life of the Church but also shape them in their faith, help them grow in love of God, and cultivate their musical talents so that they might then serve the Church with their distinct musical gifts. Only in this way can we hope to form new generations of church musicians who will be able to bring about a renaissance of sacred music within the Church, which will then affect the wider culture.

*What would you say is the relation between music, art, and moral formation?*

In art, as in the Christian life, truth, goodness, and beauty always walk together, side by side. There is no true goodness without beauty, no beauty without truth. And there is no true life without goodness and moral uprightness. Detaching or trying to isolate these elements of an inseparable unity is a sign of dishonesty—of trying to cheat art and to live a lie. The great musical works, almost in their entirety, have been composed by deeply spiritual men, who despite their flaws were able to perceive an aspect of divine beauty that they have reflected in the works of art they shared with the world. They knew how to silence the noise of man and listen to the voice of God made incarnate in artistic creations. This ability to recognize objective beauty is fundamental in journeying toward Him who is Beauty incarnate: Jesus Christ. This is why formation in beauty, especially the beauty present in music and art, constitutes a fundamental discipline for the education of children and for the continuing education of adults. And since everything that we know and experience that is good, beautiful, and true is a reflection of God, they can provide us with a foundational understanding of the nature of God and begin to lead us to the fullness of God Himself. That is why Saint Paul encourages us, saying: "Brethren, whatever is true, whatever is honorable, whatever is just, whatever is pure, whatever is lovely, whatever is gracious, if there is any excellence, if there is anything worthy of praise, think about these things" (Phil 4:8).

*How do cultural and religious traditions inform our approach to the liturgy? And how is this related to musical formation?*

It is essential to recognize that we all possess a heritage, an identity: our family, our language, our culture. This heritage plays a crucial role in our lives, teaching us how to act and how we should live with one another. Recognizing and understanding our cultural heritage makes it easier to accept and learn from the traditions of our Catholic faith. Rejecting what we have received is a misguided approach to life, cutting ourselves off from our roots. Tradition is the root that sustains us, not just in the present, but also in the future, for a tree cannot survive and flourish without strong roots.

The Church is herself a family, similar to our own families from which we have received our understanding of ourselves and our lives. In the same way that family and cultural traditions guide us in how to live together in society, the

Church teaches us how to pray and sing the praises of God together as a family. Musical training, then, is not just about music and possessing the skills of singing, but forms the heart and unites all men, women, and children, elevating them through the act of making music, a communal creation of beauty. And when this profound and mysterious beauty is united with the liturgy, it then forms humanity in the act of praising God with all of our heart, mind, soul, and strength.

One of the most notable and praiseworthy examples in the Church's history of institutionalizing the formation of sacred music has been the creation and development of choir schools. These schools have provided opportunities for young boys and girls to cultivate their musical abilities and immerse themselves in the musical tradition of the Church, forming them to pray through the power and beauty of sacred music. Where these schools have existed, they have not only assisted in ensuring the beautiful celebration of the Mass and Divine Office, but also have borne fruit in the beauty and goodness in the lives of their students. For the daily encounter with the liturgy and the beauty of sacred music has the power to transform their hearts, leading them to Christ from whom all beauty flows.

Choir schools have the opportunity to mirror beautifully the life of the early Christians, as described in Acts 2:46–47. "Day by day, attending the temple together and breaking bread in their homes, they partook of food with glad and generous hearts, praising God and having favor with all the people. And the Lord added to their number day by day those who were being saved." This is precisely what the boys and girls in choir schools experience day in and day out through their formation.

## *Singing with the Heart*

*I have observed that many of the great musicians and composers of the Western musical tradition have been former choristers—Joseph Haydn (1732–1809) and Maurice Duruflé (1902–1986), just to name a couple. And perhaps more commonly, many former choristers have become choral directors and professional musicians in their adulthood. Even our mutual friend Charles Cole, who was a child chorister at Westminster Cathedral in London, now serves as the choral director of the Schola Cantorum at the London Oratory, teaching and forming the boys and girls at the London Oratory School in the Church's tradition of sacred music.*

The work Charles Cole does at the London Oratory School is not just about teaching music to the students—which certainly forms their souls—but is more importantly about preparing them for their encounter with God in the liturgy. Their singing at the London Oratory allows them to be immersed in the Church's liturgical tradition, teaching them how to sing the praises of God not only with their voices but also with their hearts. Charles has also brought the London Oratory Schola Cantorum on pilgrimages and choir tours to Rome and various other places, giving them a wider exposure to the tradition of the Church present in different cultures and societies. This kind of formation, always rooted in prayer, truly has the power to shape a person's entire life, directing them toward Christ, leading them to become saints.

When I spoke with the boys of the Schola Cantorum in London in 2016, I told them how beautiful their singing was and that that beauty must also be reflected in how they live their lives as young disciples and witnesses of Jesus Christ. As Saint Benedict asserts, monks should sing the psalms with understanding, implying that they must unite their hearts and minds and their whole lives in the sung prayer they offer as praise. The liturgy and the singing of sacred music place us before God, making us conscious of our sins and spurring us on to greater holiness.

Talented musicians may sing beautifully, but unfortunately this is not always a reflection of virtuous lives. But if they sing not only with their voices, but with their mind and heart, they will recognize where there might be a disconnect in other parts of their lives that do not reflect the divine beauty present in the music. This is the challenge to each singer and choral director: to ensure that the music not only aligns with the aesthetic principles of beauty, but is indeed a reflection of the interior beauty and purity of their soul. If we choose to hold to sin, to vice in any areas of our lives, there is a hypocrisy present when seeking to make music of true beauty. And this duality and stubbornness can lead to a person becoming cynical, focused only on the outward appearance and the exterior criteria of beauty, when instead we must surrender ourselves completely to Christ so that the wounds of our souls might be healed by Him.

As the prophet Amos reminds us, religious celebrations should correspond to the lives of the worshipers. Exterior rites should always express our interior commitment to morality and justice. "I hate, I despise your feasts, and I take no delight in your solemn assemblies. Even though you offer me your burnt offerings and cereal offerings, I will not accept them, and the peace offerings of your fatted beasts I will not look upon. Take away from me the noise of your songs; to the melody of your harps I will not listen. But let justice roll down like waters, and righteousness like an ever-flowing stream" (Amos 5:21–24).

*This reminds me of the text of the Chorister's Prayer: "Bless, O Lord, us thy servants who minister in thy temple. Grant that what we sing with our lips we may believe in our hearts, and what we believe in our hearts we may show forth in our lives. Through Jesus Christ, Our Lord. Amen." For several years now, I have begun my own choir rehearsals with praying this prayer so that the focus on creating beautiful music does not become an end in and of itself; it should always be, first and foremost, a prayer. Sadly, it is common in professional church music circles for the hearts and lives of the musicians to be detached from the action of giving sung praise to God.*

Indeed, singing should always be an outward manifestation of the integrity of our lives, a reflection of living in harmony with God and God's laws. What we communicate to God should not be mere words or sounds, but a sincere expression of our hearts. Singing as a community has the power to foster friendship and fraternity, uniting all in one voice, as one body in Christ. If a singer has a grievance against another, he must reconcile with him, so that their voices *and their hearts* may create beauty in harmony. When hearts are in harmony, the harmony of voices will naturally follow.

*This brings us back to the vital role of music in the formation of a life of prayer, and the glorification of God through the Church's liturgical life.*

As these children grow and face the inevitable temptations of life, their rootedness in the practice of approaching Christ in the liturgy will help further convert their lives, fostering a deep love for God and a desire to serve Him throughout their entire lives.

By immersing young people in the beauty and tradition of the Church's worship, we are helping to form them as saints, so that they may be men and women of integrity. It is only in this way that they will become true musicians, artists, and leaders in whatever they do, carrying with them the gifts they have received so that they might then be able to give them to others and lead them to Christ.

## *The Tradition of Boy Choirs*

*For much of the history of the Church there has been a tradition of men's and boys' choirs, with the Sistine Chapel Choir being the most visible example of the tradition today. Vatican II, in its Constitution on the Sacred Liturgy,* Sacrosanctum concilium, *says, "Composers and singers, especially boys, must also be given a genuine liturgical training."[3] Can you explain why particular focus is given to the musical and liturgical training of boys? Is this an example of unjust discrimination toward girls? Is this related to the tradition of the Church to only ordain men to the diaconate and the priesthood?*

In order to understand the answers to these questions fully, I will first address the concern, and sometimes the accusation, that the Church unjustly discriminates against some of its members, particularly against women. The Good News of salvation that Jesus brought to save all of humanity does not discriminate. Salvation is for all, and to discriminate in this way would be antithetical to the Gospel. And in principle, the Church does not condone exclusion or discrimination toward any group of people, whether they are women or a particular ethnic or cultural group. When reading that passage from *Sacrosanctum concilium*, one must also keep in mind that the same document calls for music education in the formation of all young people, stating that "great importance is to be attached to the teaching and practice of music in seminaries, in the novitiates and houses of study

[3] Ibid., no. 115.

of religious of both sexes, and also in other Catholic institutions and schools."[4]

From the very beginning, Christ has called men and women to dedicate their lives to Him in service to the Church. However, we must also recognize that in the Gospels, Christ only called men to serve the Church as his priests, with women called to serve in other distinct and complementary ways. This is not a matter of discrimination, as to see it as such would be to adopt a worldly perspective in seeking to understand the Church. If we try to conform the Church to worldly ways of thinking, we would do well to remember the profound words of Saint Paul: "But who are you, a man, to answer back to God? Will what is molded say to its molder, 'Why have you made me thus?'" (Rom 9:20). Rather, we must humbly submit our hearts and minds to the will of Christ. When the Church continues to this day only ordaining men to sacred orders, she is obeying the tradition that Christ has established, without adding to it or taking away from it in order to suit the changeable opinions of man.

The key to understanding the perspective of the Church is provided in the writings of Saint Paul wherein he describes the complementarity of the members of the human body as analogous to the complementarity of roles within the mystical Body of Christ, the Church. The various members of the body do not vie for control of the body, as all must give themselves in service to the head, which is Christ. The Church recognizes, affirms, and honors the distinct and complementary roles that men and women have in the family, in human society, and also in the Church. Men and women are not the same, however misunderstood or

[4] Ibid.

unpopular this idea may be, and it should not be considered as unjust discrimination to recognize this fact.

The Church solemnly declares the Virgin Mary to be the "Mother of the Church", and thus the Body of Christ is her child, just as Jesus Himself is. Mary is proclaimed as "full of grace" (Lk 1:28), the "woman clothed with the sun" (Rev 12:1). Throughout the Church's history, there have been numerous examples of heroic women making significant contributions to the life and mission of the Church, such as Mary Magdalene, Saint Catherine of Siena, Saint Teresa of Avila, Saint Thérèse of Lisieux, and Saint Hildegard of Bingen. All these women have given a singular contribution to the Church's spiritual and intellectual tradition.

It is true that the cultural norms of men and women have certainly been expressed differently in various periods, often resulting in women being subject to unjust discrimination in society. In the society where Jesus lived, as well as in Greek and Roman cultures, women had different roles, freedoms, and opportunities for education. Even in the time of Shakespeare, women were not allowed to perform in theaters, with all of the roles performed by men. Cultural and economic factors have certainly played a large role in limiting the freedom of women throughout the ages. For example, throughout much of the Middle Ages, normally only royalty and those in the clergy or religious life had the economic opportunity to receive a thorough education, making the establishment of cathedral and monastic choir schools so important for the preservation of culture. The historical reality is that many of these institutions were founded to promote the education of boys, especially in their preparation for the priesthood, but there are also ample examples of monasteries for women and schools where the education of girls and women were diligently pursued.

In relation to sacred music, while the Church teaches that all men and women should receive a thorough musical education, it is especially important for boys and men to receive a proper liturgical and musical formation in order to fulfill their specific liturgical roles in accordance with the tradition of the Church. This also provides rich soil in which the vocations of those called to sacred orders can take root and grow and reap a hundredfold.

*Has not the Church in the past forbidden women from singing in liturgical choirs?*

This is an issue that requires much nuance to be fully understood. It is true that the Church has regulated the time and place for women to sing in the liturgy and that the specific rubrics governing this practice have changed at various times while the principle has remained the same, permitting all the Christian faithful to sing the praises of God in the liturgy. In the Old Testament, Miriam led the Israelite women in singing after the deliverance from the Egyptians at the Red Sea, and the New Testament hymn of Mary, the Magnificat, is prayed every evening at Vespers. Even in the early Church, a number of saints, including Saint Jerome, Saint Gregory of Nazianzus, and Saint Ambrose, speak to the beauty and appropriateness of female choirs. In the twentieth century, there has been some confusion regarding female choirs due to the following passage in Pope Saint Pius X's motu proprio *Tra le sollecitudini*:

> The liturgical chant belongs to the choir of levites, and, therefore, singers in the church, even when they are laymen, are really taking the place of the ecclesiastical choir [that is, a choir of clerics]. . . . It follows that singers in church have a real liturgical office, and that therefore women, being incapable of exercising such office, cannot be admit-

> ted to form part of the choir. Whenever, then, it is desired to employ the acute voices of sopranos and contraltos, these parts must be taken by boys, according to the most ancient usage of the Church.[5]

Following the publication of this document, it is true that many cathedrals and parishes excluded women who had previously sung in their choirs. However, this seems to me to be a misunderstanding or misapplication of the principle of liturgical singing that Pope Saint Pius X is referencing. The Schola Cantorum is the Church's fulfillment of the Old Testament's Choir of Levites, as Saint Pius X describes. And since the priesthood is reserved for men alone, the tradition of the clerical choir is also reserved for men alone. However, this should not be understood as excluding the Church's perennial use of nonclerical liturgical choirs. The Church's musical tradition has always included women in nonclerical choirs, especially those liturgical choirs in monasteries for women, in schools, and today, in parishes throughout the world. There is no contradiction in promoting the preservation of the ancient all-male clerical choir, with laymen and boys substituting for the clerics, alongside nonclerical choirs of women only or of mixed choirs of men and women or boys and girls. In clerical choirs there have certainly been abuses that the Church looks upon with great shame. In the seventeenth and eighteenth centuries, the abhorrent abuse of the *castrati*—castrating boys so that they would become men with strong high voices—was common in the professional opera world and even entered into ecclesiastical use. Thankfully, Pope Saint Pius X officially put an end to this abusive practice at the beginning of the twentieth century.

[5] Pope Pius X, motu proprio *Tra le sollecitudini* (On Sacred Music) (November 22, 1903), nos. 12–13, https://adoremus.org/1903/11/tra-le-sollecitudini.

*There are some who hold that the practice of having choirs composed solely of boys and men is no longer relevant and that they should begin to incorporate girls and/or women as an effort of providing equal opportunity. For instance, in the Anglican Church, there are a number of cathedral or collegiate choirs that have historically been male-only but in recent years have begun to incorporate girls or women. Do you think that there is still a place for all-male choirs in the Church? Should the tradition of clerical choirs consisting solely of men or men and boys be continued?*

While some of the most historic and visible liturgical choirs in the Catholic Church have been modeled on the tradition of the male-only clerical choir, in many or perhaps most places there also exist opportunities for women and girl choirs, especially in schools and parishes. And where there might not be opportunities in many cathedrals and parishes for girl choirs, or for boy choirs for that matter, in principle, the Church encourages their establishment and promotes the creation of musical opportunities and formation for both girls and boys alike. In fact, in most parishes around the world where choral singing continues to thrive, women often constitute the majority of choir members. The presence of both boy and girl choirs enriches the Church's musical heritage, each contributing a distinct beauty, and allows for a legitimate diversity of musical expression. However, I believe it would be incorrect to conclude that the existence of separate choirs for boys and girls is in and of itself unfair or unjust and that all church choirs must be mixed. Single-sex choirs have always been a part of the Church's tradition of sacred music and have a distinct and complementary value. And one of the greatest gifts of the boy choir tradition is the priestly vocations that emerge from them. Many vocations to the priesthood even today are from parishes where the liturgy and sacred music are given proper attention and care, inspiring young men in the beauty of the liturgy and in the priestly vocation. And the same is true for girls who can discern their calling to religious life in a supportive choral community of female peers. The existence of these choirs is a gift to the Church and must not be discarded in favor of mixed-only choirs. Both forms of choirs can be appropriate in certain circumstances depending on their situation, culture, and occasion (or needs) that they aim to address. Regardless, the discipline and dedication required to sing in any form of church choir can help foster a lifelong love for the Church and a desire to serve God through the gift of music. All choirs can play a vital role in the Church's liturgical life and allow men and women to use their musical talents for the glory of God and in service of the Church. And we must not forget the pastoral aspect of sacred music, for sacred music is indeed an avenue of grace, leading souls to Him through its beauty.

*As an aside, I think it is worth noting that boy choir schools are very rare in the Catholic Church today, with only one such school in the United States: Saint Paul's Choir School in Cambridge, Massachusetts. What challenges does the Church face today in forming priests who understand and value sacred music?*

Sadly, musical education for many decades has been minimal or even nonexistent in many seminaries, resulting in generations of priests ignorant of the Church's musical tradition. This is indeed ironic, since music is omnipresent in our society through modern technology. However, although "consuming" music is common today, whether in restaurants or on the train, what is less common is truly engaging with music, both in how to properly listen and how to give of oneself in making music.

Historically, seminarians were admitted to ordination only after demonstrating their ability to sing the Preface. The sung liturgy was seen as a fundamental aspect of priestly ministry, and every priest was expected to sing well or at least make a sincere effort to do so. Therefore, alongside studies in philosophy and theology, I recommend that musical education should be considered indispensable to priestly formation. Seminarians should be immersed in the Church's musical tradition, studying the great works of sacred music and learning to sing the various parts of the Mass. It is only in this way that we can hope to reverse the vicious cycle of generations of priests and bishops who have not received a thorough knowledge and appreciation of sacred music and who have consequently neglected the cultivation of sacred music in their parishes and dioceses. If we hope to witness a renewal of sacred music, we must ensure that future generations of priests receive a thorough formation in sacred music.

## *Fostering Vocations to Holiness*

*Can you speak to the role of seminaries and Catholic schools of all levels in forming saints and fostering a culture of music and art?*

The role of seminaries and Catholic schools at all levels is to form saints by teaching them to "seek first his kingdom and his righteousness" (Mt 6:33). In doing so, the cultivation of art and enrichment of culture will naturally follow, for as the Gospel promises, "all these things shall be yours as well" (Mt 6:33). As we have seen, Vatican II rightly encourages the teaching of sacred music in all schools and seminaries and encourages the founding of institutes for the promotion of sacred music whenever possible.[6]

[6] See *Sacrosanctum concilium*, no. 115.

However, one can honestly ask, "Where are the schools and institutes of sacred music that the Church has called for?" With a few very honorable exceptions there remains much work to be done for this vision to be fully implemented and realized. We must not ignore or neglect this beautiful call of the Council, but do all that we can to implement it, for from these efforts will emerge a true renewal of the liturgy and of sacred music.

Our encounter with Christ, especially in the sacred liturgy, is the fount from which all these efforts must flow. As I wrote in the *Catechism of the Spiritual Life*,

> Here we are, then, a little like Peter, James, and John after the transfiguration. We are dazzled because we have already glimpsed the divine glory, the joy of Heaven. Like Peter, we would like to say: "It is good for us to be here. Let us make three tents" (see Mt 17:4). We too want to say: let us not leave this wilderness where we have encountered Christ Jesus and where He revealed to us the Father's loving plan for us. And yet Jesus says to us, as He did to the Apostles: Do not be afraid to return to the world. Do not be afraid to return to the pagan world to proclaim the good news to it. You know now that you are not alone, but you have with you Moses, Elijah, the prophets, the Apostles, the Fathers of the Church, and the whole Communion of Saints. You know now what the source of true joy is. On your roads in exile, the sacraments will be gushing springs. Bring with you in your hearts the spirit of silence and recollection that you learned in the desert. Fear no more. You are not of the world. You are marked by the seal of Baptism; you are my children, whom I redeemed at the price of my blood.[7]

[7] Robert Cardinal Sarah, *Catechism of the Spiritual Life* (EWTN, 2022), 325.

We must understand that it is only through friendship with Christ and fidelity to His Church that we can hope for the transformation and renewal of the Church and of the culture. Our friendship with Christ must be open and visible, reflected in all aspects of our lives, and a constant invitation to the Good News of the Gospel to all we encounter. If how we live is imbued with Christ's spirit, our way of life, our culture, will be imbued with the same spirit. As Saint Paul describes, we are called to "put on Christ" (Gal 3:27; see Rom 13:14), *bringing* Christ to others by *being* Christ to others. And the same must be true in art and music—these must be imbued with the profound beauty of Him who is Beauty. And in this way, the creation and dissemination of beautiful music and art is truly part of the evangelical mission of the Church.

*I have seen firsthand how children can learn to sing the Mass and, through it, develop a love and devotion for praising God through the Church's liturgy. And this experience is certainly not limited to children, as I have heard both children and adults express feeling as though they were in heaven during the liturgy. Related to this aspect of the liturgy providing a "Transfiguration experience" for those present, how might those who direct choirs in parishes and schools seek to cultivate and foster vocations to the priesthood and the religious life, especially since the hearts and minds of the young are particularly open to instruction?*

Through the Eucharistic celebration, Christ fulfills His promise to the Church: "I am with you always, to the close of the age" (Mt 28:20). The sensory elements and the holiness of the temple help communicate this truth more clearly, forming in the faithful a foretaste of the heavenly joy. We are indeed "in heaven" whenever we truly participate in the liturgy. Although we do not yet see God "face to face" but "in a mirror dimly" (1 Cor 13:12), we are truly singing and praising God with the angels at the throne of God. This mysterious reality, far from being merely a pleasant idea or a fantasy, constitutes the very foundation of our faith. For the sacrament of the Eucharist is the rock upon which the entire Church is built. In the worship of heaven, the fullness of God's presence is revealed, no longer hidden behind the veil of the temple. The liturgy, in addition to being the "font" and "summit" of Christian life,[8] also forms and directs the soul, teaching us how to pray. The piety that the liturgy inspires in the faithful—even to the point of vocational discernment—should encourage priests, teachers, and choir directors, all of whom have no shortage of difficulties and daily crosses to carry. We are all called to behold the glory of God, to praise and adore Him, and to thank Him for all the gifts He has given us. And musicians play a vital role in helping us express our praise of the almighty God. The vocation of the church musician is one of great importance, one that involves standing before the Lord in the beauty of holiness. Whenever we sing God's praises, we are not merely singing notes and words—we are surrendering our voices, our hearts, and our lives to the praise of God. And by doing so, we become holy, just as God is holy.

[8] *Sacrosanctum concilium*, no. 10.

# Part V

# The Way of Beauty and the Way of the Cross

12

# EVANGELIZATION THROUGH BEAUTY

PETER CARTER: *Your Eminence, in our discussion of active participation, you mentioned that Saint Augustine recounted his own experience of being moved to tears at the beauty of sacred music, leading him to his conversion of life. In this example, the beauty of the liturgy also served as an invitation to conversion. Can you speak to how the sacred liturgy has the potential to evangelize through its manifestation of beauty?*

ROBERT CARDINAL SARAH: The beauty of sacred art is itself an invitation and a witness to faith in Christ. If the Church maintains artistic integrity in its sacred music, then it is a witness of beauty in the world, and that beauty points and leads us to Christ, to the fullness of truth. After I was consecrated as a bishop, a Muslim man came to me wanting his child to become a Christian, not because of any particular doctrine of the Church, but because he was profoundly touched by witnessing the beauty of the Church's liturgy.

Pope Benedict outlined three core tasks for the Church: *kerygma-martyria* (evangelization), *diakonia* (the ministry of charity), and *leitourgia* (worship of God).[1] Liturgy is intended first and foremost for praising God, not as a tool for evangelization. However, the beauty of the liturgy certainly leads people to discover God, and in this sense is a

[1] Benedict XVI, encyclical letter *Deus caritas est* (God Is Love) (December 25, 2005), no. 25.

form of evangelization, although that is not its primary purpose.

When the liturgy is celebrated beautifully, for the glory of God and for our salvation, it has a magnetism that draws people, both inside and outside of the Church. Many have been drawn to faith not through direct preaching, but because they saw something beautiful, something with integrity, and were attracted to it and wanted to be part of it. Similarly, when sacred art is created with integrity, it becomes a witness in the world, just like the sacred art of Rome today. The transition of Rome from the heart of the pagan world to the heart of the Christian Church reflects the transformative power of Christian culture, which itself is an expression of the faith of generations of Christians. This power of art to move hearts and bring people closer to Christ is not limited to sacred art alone. When I saw the movie *The Passion of the Christ* by Mel Gibson, I found it profoundly moving. Meditating on Christ's Passion in this way helped me celebrate the Eucharist more deeply, feeling more united with our Lord, and with a heightened awareness of His suffering and immense sacrifice. Even so, what we see in the film, I think, is but a glimpse of what Christ truly suffered for us. In a sense, the movie *The Passion of the Christ* can be seen as a kind of Christian enculturation, as it can help to draw us into a more intimate encounter with the mysteries of our faith. Artistic works such as films like this, Christmas pageants or Passion plays, can help incorporate the life of our Lord into our cultures, but it is important to distinguish these things from the worship of God, in which we participate in the liturgy.

When it comes to the liturgy, we must be prudent and discerning, recognizing the fundamental purpose of the liturgy, while acknowledging its potential for evangelization. It is only in this way that the integrity of the liturgy is preserved and true pastoral outreach may be accomplished. The sacred music of the liturgy must likewise first reflect the liturgy's primary purpose while also serving the secondary purpose of the edification of the faithful, drawing them into the mystery and leading them to a more profound faith. These ends are not mutually exclusive, but there is a clear distinction between them.

## *Understanding Christian Culture*

*Can you define Christian culture for us? Why does it matter?*

A religion is always embedded in a culture, as religious practice is physical as well as spiritual, just as the person is both physical and spiritual. The Lord Jesus chose to be born into an ordinary family, to have a father and mother like everyone else, to work and live in a city like all men. Thus, Jesus assimilated the culture of His time and based His message on this culture, without, however, subordinating His message to a culture, not even the Jewish one.

The culture of the Christian Church has developed and expressed itself gradually, beginning in the contexts of Jewish and Roman societies and spreading throughout the world. But since the Gospel message is transhistorical and transcultural, Christian culture, properly understood, transcends the divisions of human cultures and societies. Christ's kingdom, supernatural in essence, is grafted, incarnated, into the world but without being of the world. As Saint Paul tells us in his Letter to the Hebrews, "we have not a high priest who is unable to sympathize with our weaknesses, but one who in every respect has been tempted as we are, yet without sinning" (Heb 4:15). Therefore, every element of human cultures must be purified and sanctified and conformed to the nature of Christ, for it truly to be considered Christian culture.

The Scriptures, although expressed in human language, transcend human cultures, leading us to know and participate in the nature of God. But since our knowledge of God is imperfect, so is our language and understanding of God. The *Catechism of the Catholic Church* reminds us of this: "God transcends all creatures. We must therefore continually purify our language of everything in it that is limited, image-bound or imperfect, if we are not to confuse our image of God—'the inexpressible, the incomprehensible, the invisible, the ungraspable'—with our human representations. Our human words always fall short of the mystery of God."[2]

But at the same time, the Church of Christ is a religious body with defined characteristics—the original meaning of the word "cult"—which has produced a culture that incorporates all good things from God, most especially the sacraments instituted by Jesus Christ. Thus, the Church has a unique "Christian culture", distinct from the cultures of other religions and nations. *For this reason*, Jesus sent the Apostles not to spread and transmit a specific human culture, but to announce the Gospel and the Kingdom of God among us, thereby purifying and sanctifying the cultures of man. The Christian culture is that of God, because Christians are citizens of heaven. And the laws of God, of Christian culture, are above those established by man. Christian culture by its very nature supremely surpasses all human cultures because it is established by Christ; it is the Kingdom of God that is among us (see Lk 17:21).

[2] *Catechism of the Catholic Church*, no. 42, quoting Liturgy of Saint John Chrysostom, Anaphora.

It was in God's providence that Rome, the *caput mundi*—the *urbe* of the greatest and most powerful empire in the world—would become the seat of the Church of Christ, the Messiah awaited by the Jews and preached throughout the world. It is not by chance that Saint Peter and Saint Paul, the two pillars of the evangelization of the nascent Church, brought the Good News to the pagans of Rome and were both martyred there. These two pillars, these two lights kindled by Jesus Christ, were convinced that "the true light that enlightens every man was coming into the world" (Jn 1:9). They gave their lives to proclaim this truth, and their witness illuminated the world and Rome with the light of the Gospel and began a radical transformation of Roman culture. As the witness of the early Christian Church grew, Christianity spread rapidly as a new form of life, particularly by the time Emperor Constantine embraced the faith and allowed the public worship and freedom of the Church. The faith more fully spread throughout the earth in the fourth century, as Saint Augustine wrote, and the period has subsequently been called the Christian Era.

But what are the differences between Christians and those of other religions, between Christian culture and non-Christian cultures? The beautiful and historic *Letter to Diognetus* offers us a complete panorama:

> For Christians cannot be distinguished from the rest of the human race by country or language or customs. . . . Yet, although they live in Greek and barbarian cities alike, as each man's lot has been cast, and follow the customs of the country in clothing and food and other matters of daily living, at the same time they give proof of the remarkable and admittedly extraordinary constitution of their own commonwealth. They live in their own countries, but only as aliens. They have a share in everything as citizens, and

> endure everything as foreigners. Every foreign land is their fatherland, and yet for them every fatherland is a foreign land. . . . It is true that they are "in the flesh," but they do not live "according to the flesh." They busy themselves on earth, but their citizenship is in heaven. They obey the established laws, but in their own lives they go far beyond what the laws require. They love all men, and by all men are persecuted. They busy themselves on earth, but their citizenship is in heaven. . . . To put it simply: What the soul is in the body, that Christians are in the world. . . . The soul is shut up in the body, and yet itself holds the body together; while Christians are restrained in the world as in a prison, and yet themselves hold the world together. The soul, which is immortal, is housed in a mortal dwelling; while Christians are settled among corruptible things, to wait for the incorruptibility that will be theirs in heaven.[3]

The Christian culture is different from other cultures because its foundation is God, the Creator of every human being and their human development. Thus, based on a supernatural foundation, it reveals characteristics that no other culture possesses. Pope Francis speaks of these characteristics in his apostolic exhortation *Gaudete et exsultate*:

> We do well to keep reminding ourselves that there is a hierarchy of virtues that bids us seek what is essential. The primacy belongs to the theological virtues, which have God as their object and motive. At the center is charity, Saint Paul says that what truly counts is "faith working through love" (Gal 5:6). We are called to make every effort to preserve charity: "The one who loves another has fulfilled

[3] *The So-Called Letter to Diognetus*, in *Library of Christian Classics*, ed. John Baillie, John T. McNeill, and Henry P. Van Dusen, vol. 1, *Early Christian Fathers*, trans. and ed. Cyril C. Richardson (Westminster Press, 1953), nos. 5–8.

> the law . . . for love is the fulfillment of the law" (Rom 13:8.10). "For the whole law is summed up in a single commandment, 'You shall love your neighbor as yourself'" (Gal 5:14).[4]

No culture has ever had such a foundation, just as no religion has ever had it. When the guards who had been sent by the chief priests and the Pharisees to arrest Jesus returned—as narrated by Saint John in his Gospel—in response to the question "Why did you not bring him?", the guards answered: "No man ever spoke like this man!" (Jn 7:45–46). The differentiating element is God Himself: Christ, "the pioneer and perfecter of our faith" (Heb 12:2), who incarnates Himself in a culture and transforms it, renewing it from within. It is the "new song" of the Sacred Scriptures, the song that Christ brought into the world and into history, after which no song will ever be the same. After the Paschal Mystery of Christ, the universe changes forever, and the "new song" is its unmistakable manifestation.

There is an urgent need to know and love the Christian culture that is born from the presence of the Trinitarian God in Christ. While the message of Christ certainly reaches the human person through silent, contemplative prayer (mystics even speak of "infused contemplation" beyond the senses), the Church by its very nature as the People of God has an intrinsic communal dimension. This communal reality gives rise to a distinct culture, transformed by the leaven of Christ Himself. The Christian culture is meant actively to permeate and elevate the whole of human society, acting as the leaven that "leavens all the dough" (Gal 5:9).

[4] Francis, apostolic exhortation *Gaudete et exsultate* (On the Call to Holiness in Today's World) (March 19, 2018), no. 60.

## Via pulchritudinis: *Evangelization Through Art*

*Let's discuss the* via pulchritudinis, *the way of beauty, particularly in relation to evangelization and the role of artists. How should artists approach their work in relation to serving God and the Church?*

First we must remember that God is the source of all beauty. When we strive to imitate the beauty of God, inspired by His creation, we can attain something truly beautiful. Everything beautiful originates from God, which is a sentiment echoed by Saint Augustine. When we observe the skies, the vastness of creation, we must ask ourselves, who created all this beauty? The answer is God, for He is beautiful.

Beauty in the liturgy is not commercial in nature. It is a sacrifice, a tribute offered before God. Everything we do for God, including the creation of beauty, must originate from Him. This beauty is then given back to God to glorify His name. This is evident when we look at the Old Testament, where the vessels and ornamentation inside the Temple are described with exquisite detail. These fruits of human artistry are gifts that find their source in God and are most fittingly used in praise of Him.

In his *Letter to Artists*, Pope Saint John Paul II writes of the unique role that artists have in the life of the Church and of society:

> Society needs artists, just as it needs scientists, technicians, workers, professional people, witnesses of the faith, teachers, fathers and mothers, who ensure the growth of the person and the development of the community by means of that supreme art form which is "the art of education". Within the vast cultural panorama of each nation, artists have their unique place. Obedient to their inspiration in

> creating works both worthwhile and beautiful, they not only enrich the cultural heritage of each nation and of all humanity, but they also render an exceptional social service in favor of the common good.[5]

John Paul II makes it clear that the artistic vocation is not meant for isolation from the world, but is rather a calling to engage with and enrich society through one's artistic works. True beauty has a remarkable power to pierce hearts and awaken souls. Often people stand admiring a beautiful painting or sculpture, unaware that such artistic masterpieces were created to give glory to God. The beauty present in a church—the paintings, architecture, music—all of it serves the purpose of lifting minds and hearts to admire and contemplate Him.

In Matthew 5:16, Christ tells His disciples: "Let your light so shine before men, that they may see your good works and give glory to your Father who is in heaven." Similarly, in John 17:15–18, He says, "I do not pray that you should take them out of the world, but that you should keep them from the evil one. They are not of the world, even as I am not of the world. Sanctify them in the truth; your word is truth. As you sent me into the world, so I have sent them into the world."

Pope Saint John Paul II also highlights the self-sacrificing spirit that must imbue the life of the Christian artist:

> The particular vocation of individual artists decides the arena in which they serve and points as well to the tasks they must assume, the hard work they must endure and the responsibility they must accept. Artists who are conscious of all this know too that they must labour without allowing themselves to be driven by the search for empty glory or the

[5] John Paul II, Letter to Artists (April 4, 1999), no. 4.

craving for cheap popularity, and still less by the calculation of some possible profit for themselves. There is therefore an ethic, even a "spirituality" of artistic service, which contributes in its way to the life and renewal of a people. It is precisely this to which Cyprian Norwid seems to allude in declaring that "beauty is to enthuse us for work, and work is to raise us up".[6]

Likewise, Pope Saint Paul VI eloquently expresses the indispensable role of artists as custodians of beauty for the human race:

> This world in which we live needs beauty in order not to sink into despair. It is beauty, like truth, which brings joy to the heart of man and is that precious fruit which resists the wear and tear of time, which unites generations and makes them share things in admiration. And all of this is through your hands. May these hands be pure and disinterested. Remember that you are the guardians of beauty in the world. May that suffice to free you from tastes which are passing and have no genuine value, to free you from the search after strange or unbecoming expressions. Be always and everywhere worthy of your ideals and you will be worthy of the Church which, by our voice, addresses to you today her message of friendship, salvation, grace and benediction.[7]

## *Beauty Denotes the Presence of God*

*In your book* Catechism of the Spiritual Life, *you gave a profound insight about the power of the transcendentals: "There are some absolute values, what philosophers call the transcendentals: unity, truth, goodness, and beauty. He who perceives them, honors*

[6] Ibid., no. 4.

[7] Paul VI, Address to Artists (December 8, 1965).

*them, and loves them perceives, honors, and loves Jesus Christ, even if he does not know it, even if he considers himself an atheist, because, in reality, Christ is truth, justice, and beauty itself."*[8] *This idea is very encouraging, especially for artists, since it means that all who are involved with creating beauty and helping others to perceive and to love beautiful things are helping to bring people closer to Christ.*

The reality of transcendental values—unity, truth, goodness, and beauty—is absolute and common to all eras and cultures, elevating the art that possesses them to the level of "incarnating" these aspects of God in the creations of man, such that God's presence can be felt and experienced in them. Pope Benedict was very aware of this reality in his address to artists in the Sistine Chapel in 2009, quoting the words of Simone Weil: "In all that awakens within us the pure and authentic sentiment of beauty, there, truly, is the presence of God. There is a kind of incarnation of God in the world, of which beauty is the sign. Beauty is the experimental proof that incarnation is possible. For this reason all art of the first order is, by its nature, religious."[9]

*Because beauty present in art is an objective manifestation of God's beauty, it would seem that beautiful art can lead people to faith in Christ even when the artist may not have possessed a religious faith. The music of Gabriel Fauré and Ralph Vaughan Williams come to mind, as they both wrote beautiful liturgical music but are said to have been agnostic. Should a composition of liturgical music be judged, then, on its own artistic merits independent of the faith of the composer, or should liturgical music written by Catholics be*

[8] Robert Cardinal Sarah, *Catechism of the Spiritual Life* (EWTN, 2022), 300.

[9] See Simone Weil, *Gravity and Grace*, trans. Arthur Wills (G.P. Putnam's Sons, 1952), 153, quoted in Benedict XVI, Address at the Meeting with Artists (Sistine Chapel, November 21, 2009).

*preferred to liturgical music written by non-Catholic Christians or non-Christians?*

The mysterious presence of the Spirit "blows where it wills" (Jn 3:8) in artistic creation, and although the liturgy itself assumes and demands faith, sacred music of proven artistic and religious value can, in theory, be introduced into the liturgy as long as it properly fulfills the purpose of sacred music in the liturgy and the music and the composer is not an object of scandal. While the Church has always held up Gregorian chant and the great polyphony of the Catholic renewal era as the ideal for liturgical music, this does not mean that works composed by non-Catholics or even non-believers are to be automatically excluded. The reality of transcendental values, as absolute and common to all eras and cultures, elevates the works that arise from them to the level of "incarnation", where the Presence of God is experienced, even if the artist may not be fully aware of it.

However, we must always be mindful of the dangers that can arise when beauty is isolated from goodness and truth. Aestheticism, which pursues beauty as an end in itself, and hedonism, which seeks pleasure as the highest goal, can lead us astray from the true purpose of sacred art. To avoid these pitfalls, artists must always strive to create works that are grounded in faith, love, and service to God, allowing the beauty they create to be a reflection of the divine beauty that is the source of all true art. Beauty, when pursued as an end in and of itself, leads to a distortion of created beauty, as it should always lead us to Him who *is* Beauty.

Pope Saint John Paul II wonderfully describes this oftentimes mysterious nature of beauty: "Beauty is a key to the mystery and a call to transcendence. It is an invitation to savor life and to dream of the future. That is why the beauty of created things can never fully satisfy. It stirs that hidden nostalgia for God which a lover of beauty like Saint Augustine could express in incomparable terms: 'Late have I loved you, beauty so old and so new: late have I loved you!'"[10]

It should also be noted that faith *inspires* artistic creation. The profound communion in prayer with the Creator has always inspired our sensibilities to show forth His goodness and beauty in our own artistic creations. How many of the Church's treasured hymns were written by her saints and mystics, those who have experienced the transformative power of grace! Pope Saint John Paul II also speaks of this in his *Letter to Artists*: "How many sacred works have been composed through the centuries by people deeply imbued with the sense of the mystery! The faith of countless believers has been nourished by melodies flowing from the hearts of other believers, either introduced into the liturgy or used as an aid to dignified worship. In song, faith is experienced as vibrant joy, love, and confident expectation of the saving intervention of God."[11]

## *Beauty Without Goodness and Truth*

*As you mentioned, there are certain risks associated with the study and pursuit of beauty when detached from the other transcendentals of goodness and truth: aestheticism, where beauty alone becomes the ultimate goal of art, and hedonism, where pleasure alone becomes the goal. How can these risks be mitigated, particularly for musicians who dedicate their lives to studying and promoting beauty in service to the truth?*

[10] John Paul II, Letter to Artists, no. 16. Original footnote: "Sero te amavi! Pulchritudo tam antiqua et tam nova, sero te amavi!: *Confessions*, 10, 27: CCL 27, 251."

[11] Ibid., no. 12.

At the heart of this question lies a fundamental issue of the precise meaning of these words. What is beauty? And what, indeed, is pleasure? Would an inhabitant of ancient Greece have a different concept of beauty from a contemporary Chinese person or a nineteenth-century French person? Is it even possible to have an objective discernment on this matter? The Church responds that having an objective discernment of beauty is indeed possible: One can know, in reality, what beauty is, even if one's ability to perceive it is limited. However, it is crucial to understand that the term "beautiful" according to solely worldly values differs from the Christian concept, which posits that all created beauty is a reflection of the beauty of God, especially of Christ, who is Beauty incarnate. A similar phenomenon can be found in the case of terms like "pleasure" or "freedom". The pleasure that arises from hedonism is not the same as the "sweet intoxication of the Spirit", just as Christian "freedom", arising from the truth of God, has no relation to an unfounded idea of freedom capable of leading to forms of anarchy.

Pope Benedict reflects on the Christian understanding of art in his essay *Sing Artistically for God*:

> According to the Christian faith . . . it belongs to the essence of human beings that they come from God's "art," that they themselves are a part of God's art and as perceivers can think and view God's creative ideas with him and translate them into the visible and the audible. If this be the case, then to serve is not foreign to art; only by serving the Most High does it exist at all. . . . It is precisely the test of true creativity that the artist steps out of the esoteric circle and knows how to form his or her intuition in such a way that the others—the many—may perceive what the artist has perceived. In the process, the three conditions for true art specified in the book of Exodus are always valid: artists

> must be moved by their hearts; they must have understanding, that is, be skillful people; and they must have perceived what the Lord himself has shown.[12]

*The Book of Ecclesiastes seems to take a rather pessimistic view of human endeavors: "Vanity of vanities! All is vanity. What does man gain by all the toil at which he toils under the sun?" (Eccles 1:2–3). How can we know that our efforts to build up the musical and artistic culture of the Church are not merely an exercise in the futility of human activity?*

Being in the presence of God and worshiping Him with due praise is the opposite of vanity; it is a source of profound humility. However, we must be cautious, as a certain "aestheticism" or dangerous self-referentiality could lead us to create or take pleasure in empty works, devoid of meaning because they are divorced from their very origin and purpose. When art, or indeed all human activity, seeks to negate or avoid its ultimate purpose of serving and praising God, it truly is an exercise of vanity, as Ecclesiastes describes. This is nowhere more evident than in the deceptive and injurious view that art should be pursued, created, and loved, solely for "art's sake". Pope Benedict XVI warns us against this view, reminding us that the nature of art is to serve:

> First of all, that hybrid aestheticism which excludes every function of art as service, that is, which can only regard art as having its own purpose and its own standard, is incompatible with the directives of the Bible. Wherever it is exhibited consistently this presumptuousness necessarily leads to a nihilistic lack of standards and therefore generates nihilistic parodies of art, but not a new creativity. The

[12] Pope Benedict XVI (Joseph Ratzinger), "Sing Artistically for God", in *A New Song for the Lord: Faith in Christ and Liturgy Today* (Crossroad Publishing Company, 2013), 133–34.

> philosophy at work here belies the creaturely determination of the human being; it would like to elevate the human person to the level of a pure creator. But in this way it leads the human person into untruth, into contradiction with his or her own nature; untruth, however, always drifts into the disintegration of what is creative. Earlier we had briefly touched on the problematic nature of the modern concept of creativity in which the anthropological problem of the modern age is present in a concentrated way. In idealistic philosophy the human spirit is no longer primarily receptive—it does not receive, but is only productive. In the existential radicalization of this approach, nothing meaningful at all precedes human existence. The human being comes from a meaningless factuality and is thrown into a meaningless freedom. The person thus becomes a pure creator; at the same time his or her creativity becomes a mere whim and, precisely for this reason, empty.[13]

Pope John Paul II also cautions against the idolization of the artist and the artistic creation:

> True artists above all are ready to acknowledge their limits and to make their own the words of the Apostle Paul, according to whom "God does not dwell in shrines made by human hands" so that "we ought not to think that the Deity is like gold or silver or stone, a representation by human art and imagination" (Acts 17:24, 29). If the intimate reality of things is always "beyond" the powers of human perception, how much more so is God in the depths of his unfathomable mystery![14]

Both popes emphasized that art must serve a higher purpose and that artists must acknowledge their limits and the transcendent reality beyond human perception and artistic

[13] Ibid., 133.

[14] John Paul II, Letter to Artists, no. 6.

creation. When art departs from the transcendental values, it constitutes a clear sign that the artist is distanced from true art, which is always an act of love and communication—of communion—not an end in itself, which is when it becomes an idol. In this way, faith does not diminish art but exalts it and encourages us to contemplate its ultimate goal, which is God Himself.

Our efforts in sacred music and art should serve as a constant reminder of the heavenly liturgy that awaits us. We must go forth with renewed zeal and devotion, seeking to create and promote a culture of beauty within the Church, a beauty that always points to the source of all beauty, which is God Himself. My advice is to focus on that which is within our control: to carry out the liturgical actions in the best possible manner, humbly following the Church's liturgical rubrics and without neglecting anything relating to the holiness of the temple—sacred music, sacred art, sacred silence, gestures—and having all these things be an expression of our hearts. At the same time, where there exist problems outside of our control—whether in regard to the liturgy, the governance of the Church, or anything else—we must persevere in faith and hope, being mindful of our Lord's promise that He will never abandon His Church, and constantly praying that His "will be done on earth as it is in heaven" (Mt 6:10).

When we pray and sing the liturgy with integrity, whether or not we personally possess a beautiful voice, we are truly joining our voices with the choirs of angels in praise of God. In this light, we can see that the pursuit of beauty in sacred music is not a vain or futile endeavor, but rather an expression of love and a true participation in the heavenly liturgy. As Pope Benedict XVI wrote in his *Spirit of the Liturgy*:

> The singing of the Church comes ultimately out of love. It is the utter depth of love that produces the singing. "*Cantare amantis est*", says St. Augustine, singing is a lover's thing. In so saying, we come again to the trinitarian interpretation of Church music. The Holy Spirit is love, and it is he who produces the singing. He is the Spirit of Christ, the Spirit who draws us into love for Christ and so leads to the Father.[15]

And speaking directly to artists, he exhorts them: "Be grateful, then, for the gifts you have received and be fully conscious of your great responsibility to communicate beauty, to communicate in and through beauty! Through your art, you yourselves are to be heralds and witnesses of hope for humanity! And do not be afraid to approach the first and last source of beauty, to enter into dialogue with believers, with those who, like yourselves, consider that they are pilgrims in this world and in history towards infinite Beauty!"[16]

In summary, we can see that the praise of God, and the building up of the musical and artistic culture of the Church is not a vain or futile work when undertaken with the right disposition of the heart and given as a true offering to God. It is indeed a noble and essential task that artists use their gifts to create works of beauty that point to God, the ultimate source of all beauty. And since music is indeed integral to the liturgy, investing in the musical formation and support of musicians becomes essential to the liturgical life and pastoral care of a parish. We have a solemn duty to provide for the worthy worship of almighty God and to nurture the gifts He has bestowed upon those called to serve Him

[15] Joseph Cardinal Ratzinger, *The Spirit of the Liturgy* (Ignatius Press, 2000), 142.

[16] Benedict XVI, Address of His Holiness Benedict XVI at the Meeting with Artists (Sistine Chapel, November 21, 2009).

through music. We must always be vigilant that artistic endeavors remain grounded in humility, love, and service to God and His Church, without succumbing to the temptations of pursuing beauty and art for its own sake.

# 13

# SUPPORTING THE CULTURE OF BEAUTY IN THE CHURCH

PETER CARTER: *Those who want to foster and support the musical culture of the Church are often dismayed when they realize the degree of effort and financial resources that it requires. And with so many pressing and competing needs in the world, some might question whether sacred music should be a priority for the Church. How would you respond to the argument that the Church should instead primarily focus its resources on her charitable activities such as education, healthcare, and serving the poor?*

ROBERT CARDINAL SARAH: For the answer to this question we need to look no further than to the example of Christ in the Gospel. When Jesus visited Lazarus in Bethany before His Passion, Mary anointed His feet with expensive oil. Jesus graciously received this humble and profound gesture, while Judas criticized it as a waste, since the oil could have been sold and the money given to the poor. Christ reprimanded him to leave her alone, for "The poor you always have with you, but you do not always have me" (Jn 12:8). From this example, we must accept that it is only right and just to praise and worship God in a fitting manner, not with dirty or worn-out garments but by offering the best of what we have, just as the Levites did in the Old Testament, and as Abel did in the book of Genesis. Not with blemished or defective animals for sacrifice—as if disposing of something unwanted—but truly with the best of our first fruits, even as God the Father sacrificed His Son for our salvation. And while Christ says that the poor are always with you, He also teaches us that whatever we do for the least of our brothers and sisters, we do for Him (see Mt 25:40). There is no contradiction in this. Love for God and love for our neighbor are the two great commandments on which hang the whole Law and the Prophets (see Mt 22:37–40). The Second Vatican Council teaches that "the liturgy is the summit toward which the activity of the Church is directed; at the same time it is the font from which all her power flows",[1] and Saint Paul reminds us that without charity, we are nothing more than a "noisy gong or a clanging cymbal" (1 Cor 13:1). Thus, we praise God in the liturgy, and we also praise Him through acts of fraternal love and mercy.

Mother Teresa of Calcutta understood that there are many different kinds of poverty in the world today. In wealthy countries, she witnessed the spiritual poverty, the loneliness and despair of many people, and saw its devastating effects on the soul. Stripping the liturgy of all art and beauty, of what is proper to it, betrays a reductive mentality that is foreign to the nature of the liturgy and undoubtedly leads to an even greater poverty, as it fails to bring forth its immense richness, both materially in terms of sacramental signs, and spiritually in terms of the realities to which these signs point. The liturgy is the greatest treasure that the Church possesses on earth, a reflection and foretaste of the heavenly liturgy.

When we witness the spiritual misery present in affluent countries, the grave moral and anthropological crises, the doctrinal confusion, and the indifference toward God and His teachings, we would do well to remember that the

[1] Vatican Council II, Constitution on the Sacred Liturgy *Sacrosanctum concilium* (December 4, 1963), no. 10.

Church approaches spiritual and physical poverty—indeed her whole evangelical mission—as first and foremost an act of love of God and our neighbor, not seeing her mission as just to reduce suffering or physical poverty like a non-governmental organization. Pope Saint Paul VI reminds us of this in his apostolic exhortation *Evangelii nuntiandi*:

> The work of evangelization presupposes in the evangelizer an ever increasing love for those whom he is evangelizing. That model evangelizer, the Apostle Paul, wrote these words to the Thessalonians, and they are a program for us all: "With such yearning love we chose to impart to you not only the gospel of God but our very selves, so dear had you become to us." What is this love? It is much more than that of a teacher; it is the love of a father; and again, it is the love of a mother. It is this love that the Lord expects from every preacher of the Gospel, from every builder of the Church. A sign of love will be the concern to give the truth and to bring people into unity. Another sign of love will be a devotion to the proclamation of Jesus Christ, without reservation or turning back.
>
> Yet another sign of love will be the effort to transmit to Christians not doubts and uncertainties born of an erudition poorly assimilated but certainties that are solid because they are anchored in the Word of God. The faithful need these certainties for their Christian life; they have a right to them, as children of God who abandon themselves entirely into His arms and to the exigencies of love.[2]

In the Gospel of Saint Matthew, Jesus refers to the scribes and Pharisees as hypocrites, "for you tithe mint and dill and cummin, and have neglected the weightier matters of the law, justice and mercy and faith; these you ought to have

[2] Paul VI, apostolic exhortation *Evangelii nuntiandi* (Evangelization in the Modern World) (December 8, 1975), no. 79.

done, without neglecting the others" (Mt 23:23). We must take these words to heart today and examine our own consciences and indeed the mission of the Church, making sure that we are not neglectful of any good works, but also "the weightier matters of the law, justice and mercy and faith". And because the greatest expression of our faith is the sacred liturgy, the Church and faithful lay men and women must not hesitate to do all that they can to foster and support the sacred arts—especially that of sacred music, since it is an integral part of the liturgy.

## *Working for the Church*

*Oftentimes, lay people working for the Church, whether as musicians or artists or in some auxiliary capacity, are treated as pious workers who should work primarily out of religious devotion and not expect their work to be financially compensated in a comparable way to similar work in the secular world. How should we look to those who devote their careers to service to the Church, especially since supporting the sacred arts and developing the musical culture of the Church is part of her duty to worship God with due praise?*

The teaching of the Church is clear concerning the dignity both of work and of the worker, as well as the duty of the employer to provide a just and living wage. And when the Church herself is the employer, there should be no double standard, but rather this teaching should be lived and taught in an exemplary way. In the Church's landmark document of her social teaching, *Rerum novarum*, Pope Leo XIII describes the duties of the employer:

> The following duties bind the wealthy owner and the employer: not to look upon their work people as their bondsmen, but to respect in every man his dignity as a person

ennobled by Christian character. They are reminded that, according to natural reason and Christian philosophy, working for gain is creditable, not shameful, to a man, since it enables him to earn an honorable livelihood; but to misuse men as though they were things in the pursuit of gain, or to value them solely for their physical powers—that is truly shameful and inhuman. Again justice demands that, in dealing with the working man, religion and the good of his soul must be kept in mind.[3]

Just as the Levitical priests in the Old Testament lived from their service to the Temple and had no land of their own, so too do church musicians, although most frequently not priests or religious themselves, dedicate their skills, talents, and industry to the service of the Church and the worship of God. To deprive any worker of his just wages is a grave sin—one that cries to heaven for vengeance—and pastors must earnestly examine their consciences in this regard, lest those they seek to serve are turned away from the Church by experiencing hypocrisy and scandal. The call of the Christian to give of themselves gratuitously, especially to the primary duties of their vocation, should in no way conflict with the duties of the employer to treat workers justly and with due respect. Bishops and priests should recognize that sacred music is not an optional luxury or expense, but a necessity for the Church to fulfill her mission of worship and evangelization, and that those who dedicate themselves to this noble work deserve to be supported and compensated justly, in accordance with the Church's social teaching. Indeed, the work of building up the Church's musical and artistic culture requires much effort and sacrifice,

[3] Leo XIII, encyclical letter *Rerum novarum* (On Capital and Labor) (May 15, 1891), no. 20.

but is filled with joy when undertaken out of love for God and neighbor.

Let us carefully reflect: what are we offering to the Lord in the liturgy? We must remember that in the Holy Mass, bread and wine are truly transformed into the Body and Blood of Jesus Christ, offered to the Father for the salvation of the world. We must keep in mind that the Mass is truly heaven on earth! If we recall the faith of the early Christians who were willing to suffer and lay down their lives for their faith in Christ, we will desire to offer the very best of ourselves to God in worship, including in the realm of liturgical music. It cannot be something third-rate and artless, the left-over scraps of artistic endeavors and human genius. This can only be deemed sufficient if we believe, contrary to the teachings of the Second Vatican Council, that music is *not* integral to the liturgy.[4] Artistic excellence and beauty must not be reserved for the secular world, but must shine like a beacon, inviting all into the Church to behold, just like the Paschal candle at the Easter Vigil. Indeed, if the Church does *not* lead with beauty, then it is her evangelical mission that suffers, and the great treasure of the Church's musical tradition is in grave danger of being forgotten and lost.

If we truly desire a renewal of the sacred liturgy, the Church must commit herself to reclaiming her artistic heritage, fostering and supporting artists who work to beautify her liturgy and communicate her salvific mission. As in any field, being a proficient church musician requires extensive training and expertise, and the Church must encourage and support those who wish to serve the Lord with their artistic gifts, recognizing that building up the musical culture of any parish and community demands significant ef-

[4] See *Sacrosanctum concilium*, no. 112.

fort and resources. And the artists themselves must be men and women of prayer, inspired by their encounter with the Lord, who seek to invest their talents in the vineyard of the Lord in humble service. In this way, the artist is inspired by the encounter with Him who is Beauty, and their artistic creation becomes a truly beautiful expression of praise and adoration.

We need only look to the Church's artistic history to see examples of how the flourishing of the sacred arts has been accomplished. In the Middle Ages, choir schools and choral foundations were established at cathedrals such as at Notre-Dame Cathedral in Paris and Saint Stephen's Cathedral in Vienna, and collegiate institutions such as at Oxford and Cambridge Universities, ensuring that the divine praises were sung daily in the Mass and the Divine Office. Many of these foundations were financially endowed by wealthy lay nobles who sought to give of their wealth in support of the Church, asking for prayers on their behalf. Patronage, which has marked a flourishing era in sacred art, remains a valid solution wherever possible in the efforts to revive the musical culture of the Church.

## *Patronage and Philanthropy for Sacred Music and the Arts*

*Can you discuss this idea of patronage further, and philanthropy's significance in supporting sacred music initiatives and programs? What would you say to those with financial means about the importance of supporting these types of endeavors?*

Since music is integral to the liturgy, supporting liturgical choirs and the formation of people in sacred music is also integral to supporting the Church. We must recognize that talents need nurturing, and that many families cannot afford to support this on their own. The local Church and community should identify the interested and gifted members among them, encourage them, and support their formation, as these gifts come from God Himself and must be nurtured to fully reap their fruits. A particularly talented young singer or organist from a family of limited means should ideally be able to receive scholarships to develop his talents, especially when given in service to the Church. To achieve this, we must involve the entire community—the whole *ecclesia*—in supporting these efforts. We must remember that constructing the infrastructure to praise God requires us to put the act of praising Him first. Just as building a physical church often involves substantial fundraising upfront, we must not forget that those who lead us in worship are the living stones of the Church, and they require ongoing support and formation. The same principle applies to supporting our parish priests and all those who work to produce a beautiful liturgy. They need and deserve our support. In the organization of the parish, it is essential that the budget prioritize the celebration of the liturgy with the utmost beauty and reverence. This includes allocating funds for personnel, purchasing and maintaining a parish organ, and providing adequate space for rehearsals.

Philanthropy plays a crucial role in supporting sacred music, from the most renowned institutions to the smallest parish that may be developing a choir for the first time. Whenever we help to support and cultivate the musical formation and education of people, young and old, we are helping them give praise to God Himself and investing in the very heart of the Church's worship. And our contributions, no matter how small, can truly help transform the lives of those who are learning how to "worship the LORD in the beauty of holiness" (Ps 96:6, KJV) as well as draw in all of the faithful to participate more fully in the liturgy. In this way, we are helping to ensure that the liturgy is celebrated with the proper dignity and reverence it deserves, and that future generations of musicians are formed to lead the faithful in offering praise to God.

14

# THE CROSS AS THE HOPE FOR RENEWAL

PETER CARTER: *Your Eminence, some people today feel that the Church needs to change her organizational structures so as to better fulfill her mission of fostering greater holiness among the faithful. What is your reaction to this idea?*

ROBERT CARDINAL SARAH: The Church is the mystical body of Christ, and as such, is in essence pure and holy. Our duty as Christians, as members of this body, is to conform ourselves to the image of Christ, and Christ gave us the means to this through His institution of the sacraments. The only sure way forward is to "seek first his kingdom and his righteousness" and everything else of secondary goodness will be given to us as well (Mt 6:33). We accomplish this first and foremost through encountering Christ in the liturgy where we present ourselves to Him in humble worship and open ourselves to His transformative grace and love. The crises of today do not demand the institution of a new sacrament, a new technology, or a restructuring of the Church. Holiness is achieved not through constant innovation or external change, but through growing in love for Christ and His Church. In this way, we must bear our sufferings with the same patience and love that Christ possessed in His Passion and death, and in like manner, our sufferings will bear fruit and bring live-giving grace that will be the seeds of true renewal in the Church.

*How should the faithful understand the true meaning of liturgical renewal, especially in light of the intense debates surrounding the liturgy since the Second Vatican Council?*

Despite the many changes to the Church's liturgy in the twentieth century, I think that the proper way to truly understand liturgical renewal is not to think primarily about changes in the way we pray or in the way we express ourselves as the Church. Rather, it is about returning to the source of our communion with God and allowing ourselves to be wholly converted to Him. We must adhere to the unique salvific way of the Church, the way of Christ, and follow His teachings with humility and grace. The liturgy leads us to be holy. In the presence of God, who is truly and substantially present in the liturgy, the world stands in silence before its Creator: We are called to contemplate Him with awe, reverence, humility, and praise. When we are holy, then we are able to praise and adore God, singing with our whole beings, not only with our lips or voices, but with our whole hearts. We cannot become holy in isolation, but only in unity with the Body of Christ, the Church united in our worship of God.

The liturgy is not a matter of subjective feelings or personal or cultural expressions, but an encounter with the origin of all objective reality—the reality of God Himself. Proper liturgical formation, then, should promote that which makes us holy and enables us to honor and adore God with due praise, conforming us to His likeness. It is not ultimately about changing the prayers of the Mass or adapting sacred Scripture to suit our own desires, preferences, and emotions. Our call is to give of ourselves completely to the praise of God, leaving aside all human cleverness and selfish desires, and being completely transformed by the grace of the sacraments.

## *Keeping Our Eyes Fixed on Christ*

*Many people today are disheartened and troubled by the many scandals and problems within the Church, frequently leading to anger, frustration, and discouragement. One of my favorite quotes, from the bookmark of Saint Teresa of Avila, warns against this: "Let nothing trouble you, / Let nothing scare you, / All is fleeting, / God alone is unchanging / Patience / Everything obtains. / Who possesses God / Nothing wants, / God alone suffices."*[1] Without making light of scandals and injustices, how can we maintain our focus on Christ amid these trials?

It is indeed easy to become fixated on the scandals and problems within the Church, whether they be doctrinal confusion, moral failures, scandals of a sexual nature, or hypocrisy. However, when we focus excessively on these issues instead of on Christ, we risk losing sight of what is most important. We must remember that all earthly troubles are passing, and that the crosses we are called to bear are given to us ultimately through love, so that we might be purified and strengthened and conformed to the image of Christ. The burden of our cross is not eternal, but must be daily borne with patience and hope for the day of the resurrection.

At times, we may be tempted to focus our efforts on changing only the external factors in the Church or the world, rather than doing the hard work of interior conversion. When we attend Mass, for example, we may find it easy to criticize any perceived lack of beauty or sacredness, whether in the music, the vestments, or the manner of liturgical celebration. And while it is important to strive for beauty and reverence in the liturgy, we cannot allow these concerns to distract us from the heart of the matter—our

[1] Saint Teresa of Avila, *Collected Works*, trans. Kieran Kavanaugh, O.C.D. and Otilio Rodrigues, O.C.D., 2nd ed. (ICS Publications, 1987), 386.

encounter with Christ in the sacraments. Our participation in the liturgy must lead to holiness, not division and argumentation. The liturgy, when lived properly, helps us attain holiness because it brings us face-to-face with God. In this encounter, the light of God penetrates our being, transforming us and making us holy like Him. This transformation does not come about by constantly changing things, whether creating new liturgies or reforming existing ones. Rather, it is the result of our openness to God's grace and our willingness to be conformed to His will. Whether the liturgy is celebrated with great solemnity or in humble simplicity, in a magnificent cathedral or a poor parish church, our focus must remain on Christ, who gives Himself to us fully and without reserve in all of the liturgical rites of the Church.

In our pursuit of holiness, we are called to redirect our attention to Christ constantly, especially when it is difficult. The news and scandals of the world can be addictive, tempting us to dwell on sin and darkness rather than the light of Christ. Yet, it is precisely in times of trial and suffering that we must keep our eyes fixed on the cross, uniting our own struggles with the Passion of our Lord. Nobody enjoys suffering and death for its own sake, but the liturgy leads us to die with Christ so that we too may rise with Him in glory. We may not want to suffer, but it is through suffering that we come to understand the way of salvation.

The priest, in celebrating the liturgy, must conform himself to the liturgical rubrics that the Church asks of him, not what he devises of his own accord, even if well intentioned. The temptation for the priest is to do what he may personally prefer or what people might enjoy, lowering the liturgy to the level of personal preference, rather than bringing himself and the faithful into the profound mystery of the heavenly liturgy. When we focus on our own likes and dislikes, we risk losing sight of the true essence of liturgy. And while priests, religious, and laity all have distinct callings and vocations, the fundamental path to holiness remains the same for all: Jesus Christ and the sacraments. It is not for us to decide our own way to achieve holiness; Christ Himself is "the way, and the truth, and the life" (Jn 14:6) and gives us His grace through His Church. When the people of Israel left Egypt, God guided them to Mount Sinai. But afterward, they crafted their own god to carry with them, because they wanted a deity they could control rather than allowing themselves to be led by the true God. The same temptation exists today—we want to dictate to God what the Church should be and create ways to achieve holiness through our own imaginings. But the Church is already a gift from God, and since Christ abides in her, she is holy. How can we presume to change what Christ has given to us? Certainly, we should strive for beauty, reverence, and fidelity in the liturgy. But we must not allow our personal opinions and tastes to distract us from the heart of the matter: the mystical encounter with Christ. Let us keep our eyes fixed on Him, allowing His grace to transform us from within.

## *Reform or Revolution*

*This reminds me of historical examples of divergent ways of addressing scandals. For example, during the Protestant Revolution, "reformers" like Martin Luther cut themselves off from the Church and from the valid celebration of the sacraments, proposing what they saw as a "simplified and purified" Christianity that placed its focus only on the Scriptures in isolation from Christian tradition. In contrast, we have the example of Saint Francis of Assisi, who lived several centuries before Luther, and who, like Luther, was deeply troubled by the scandals and corruption he witnessed within the Church.*

*However, his response was markedly different from Luther's in that instead of seeking to create a new church or to reform the existing one according to his own ideas, Francis embraced a life of radical commitment to Christ, and pursued holiness through living the Gospel to the fullest within the context of the Church's tradition.*

This is the key difference between Saint Francis of Assisi and Luther: While Luther sought to change the Church according to his own vision, interpreting Holy Scripture in his own way, Saint Francis allowed himself to be changed by Christ, truly living the Gospel message and seeking to heal and purify the Church while maintaining unity with her. Saint Francis did not merely preach the Gospel; he lived it integrally, embracing a life of pure poverty and holiness as taught by Jesus Christ Himself. He made himself poor to enrich us with his poverty, and amid his efforts to imitate Christ so completely, he was granted the extraordinary grace of receiving the stigmata, the marks of Christ's Passion, in his own body. The stigmata was a divine gift and special grace, a tangible sign of Francis' profound union with the crucified Lord.

God is faithful, and in order to imitate Him, we too must profess and live out our fidelity to Him and to the Church He founded. We are called to be faithful to the end, not inventing new doctrines or practices, but holding fast to what we have received: the faith of the Apostles, the teachings of the Church Fathers, the guidance of the Magisterium, and the leadership of the Holy Father, the successor of Saint Peter. There is no other way, no "new" path to holiness apart from the way that Christ has given to us through His Church. We cannot choose our own path to holiness; rather, we must allow ourselves to be guided and led by Christ. He has clearly indicated the way we must go: the way of the sacraments, the way of baptism. As He said, "He who believes and is baptized will be saved" (Mk 16:16). He did not say, "You can choose your own way to be saved." No, the path to salvation is the one that Christ has marked out for us, and it is by persevering on this path to the very end that we will be saved. The response of holiness to scandals and false teaching is to bear these crosses with patience, love, and fidelity. As Christ Himself teaches us, "If any man would come after me, let him deny himself and take up his cross and follow me" (Mt 16:24).

## *Communion That Transcends Words*

*In* God or Nothing, *you recount your profound friendship with Brother Vincent-Marie of the Resurrection, a young canon, who, even as he was dying of multiple sclerosis and had lost the ability to speak, radiated Christ's joy and peace. Your communion with him, which transcended verbal communication, is a beautiful reflection of the deep, spiritual bond we as Christians are called to have with Christ, and with one another in the Church. Can you discuss this idea of communion that transcends the ordinary means of communication?*

Often in life, we spend so much time talking, explaining, and commenting on lesser goods that we entirely miss the greatest good, *God*, and the essence of our communion with Him, a communion that transcends words. Sometimes we even speak and pray as if we create communion with God of our own accord, rather than opening ourselves to God and allowing the Holy Spirit to pray within us: "The Spirit helps us in our weakness; for we do not know how to pray as we ought, but the Spirit himself intercedes for us with sighs too deep for words" (Rom 8:26).

And the liturgy properly celebrated helps us cultivate interior silence, so we can listen to the Holy Spirit praying within us. We do not learn to pray through endless commentary or instruction, but by allowing the Spirit to pray within us. And through our reception of Holy Communion, we "put on the Lord Jesus Christ" (Rom 13:14). As Saint Augustine said: "If you receive [the Eucharist] well, you are yourselves what you receive."[2] Therefore, the way we live, speak, and behave must be an expression of the Son of God. The Spirit of God dwells in our souls, not to change doctrines or the structure of the Church, but to call everyone to holiness and conversion of life.

*The saints demonstrate a deep integration of the liturgy and the sacraments into their daily lives and spiritual practices. How can we, in our own way, follow their example and persevere on the path to holiness, even amid the trials and sufferings we encounter?*

In the lives of the saints we often find the spiritual practices such as daily Mass, frequent confession (often weekly), and the devout praying of the Church's Divine Office and various religious devotions. These are the daily habits of prayer that enabled them to take up their cross daily and follow the example of Christ. Just as an athlete must train rigorously each day to become strong, so too must the Christian integrate private prayer, the liturgy, and the sacraments into his daily life and leave behind every attachment to sin. As Saint Paul reminds us, "Since we are surrounded by so great a cloud of witnesses, let us also lay aside every weight, and

[2] Saint Augustine, "Sermon 227", in *The Works of Saint Augustine: A Translation for the 21st Century*, trans. Edmund Hill, O.P., ed. John E. Rotelle, O.S.A., pt. 3, *Sermons*, vol. 6, *Sermons 184–229Z* (New City Press, 1993), 254.

sin which clings so closely, and let us run with perseverance the race that is set before us" (Heb 12:1).

For the laity whose states in life may necessitate that their participation in the Mass is less frequent, even limited to only their Sunday obligation, the path to holiness may appear to be more challenging since they are less frequently united with the liturgy, the *opus Dei*. However, God calls all souls to holiness, regardless of the duties of their state of life. Achieving true holiness is indeed possible for all through God's grace, and we will receive the graces necessary for this if we humbly ask for them in prayer. As Christ teaches us, prayer and fasting are the two means by which demons are cast out and health restored to our souls. Fasting, in particular, has been largely forgotten or even "canceled" in many corners of the Church today. It is painful and difficult to deny ourselves in this way. But without fasting, we will struggle indefinitely to overcome the devil and his temptations, which will otherwise linger in our lives indefinitely. We must all commit to renewing the practice of fasting in our lives, whether from food, technology, or anything else that may become an idol in our lives. Fasting is a way of denying ourselves, and we must take up this cross and embrace it, letting go of every attachment that holds us back from fully "putting on Christ".

However, as we practice mortification of the flesh and desires, we must remember that growth in holiness is not a matter of merely stamping out vice, but of actively pursuing virtue. We must turn away from all that is evil and nourish ourselves with beauty and truth. We must replace what is evil with what is good by actively cultivating habits of prayer, goodness, and charity. As Saint Paul exhorts us, "Whatever is true, whatever is honorable, whatever is just, whatever is pure, whatever is lovely, whatever is gracious, if there is any excellence, if there is anything worthy of praise, think about these things" (Phil 4:8). The pain of sacrificing all lesser goods is the price we pay for seeking the highest good, and the suffering felt is the birthing pangs of building a beautiful culture that truly reflects the goodness and beauty of God. Through this sanctifying suffering we are slowly conformed to the image of Christ, allowing His light to shine through us and all that we do. And it is especially through the liturgy, the most beautiful act of Christ's sacrifice on this earth, that we are nourished, supported, and drawn further into the pursuit of holiness.

The truly great reformers of the Church began by reforming themselves in imitating Christ. And so I charge all of you who want to renew and restore the liturgical life of the Church to reform your own lives in imitation of Christ and according to the liturgy of the Church. Do what is possible according to the duties of your state of life: Attend Mass beyond your Sunday obligation, make praying parts of the Liturgy of the Hours part of your daily prayers, and learn to sing the psalms and hymns of the Church with heartfelt praise and adoration! Do not think that you can accomplish more by praying less! "But seek first his kingdom and his righteousness, and all these things shall be yours as well" (Mt 6:33).

## *The Pursuit of Beauty and the Pursuit of Holiness*

*How does the pursuit of beauty in the arts relate to the Christian pursuit of holiness?*

Just as an artist seeks to create works of excellence and beauty, so too are we as Christians called to shed all that is not good and beautiful in our souls, allowing the light of

Christ to shine completely through us. As I have described before, when artists dedicate themselves to the pursuit of beauty and artistic creation, they are ultimately pursuing the source of all beauty and participating in the creative genius of man, who is made in the image and likeness of God. The beauty in their artistic creations truly becomes a reflection of the divine beauty, a means by which others can encounter the ineffable mystery of the beauty and presence of God. The experiences of beauty in art and culture are truly avenues of grace that elevates the soul, ever leading and pointing toward the transcendent mystery of God.

Growth in holiness is a process of purification, of allowing ourselves to be stripped of all that is not of God, so that we may be filled with His grace and transformed into His likeness. This is the work of a lifetime, a daily dying to self so that Christ may live more fully in us. Art, then, can be seen as an imitation of holiness, a mirroring of Christ's incarnation. Just as Christ took on human flesh to reveal the face of God to the world, so too does the artist seek to incarnate the Divine through the medium of his art. In this way, the artist becomes a vessel of God's beauty, a channel through which His light can shine forth into the world. Of course, this is no easy task. The pursuit of beauty, both in art and in the soul, requires great sacrifice and perseverance. It is a birthing process, one that is often accompanied by pain and struggle. But it is precisely through this suffering that new life emerges, a culture and a soul that are more fully conformed to the image of Christ. In the end, the goal of both art and the spiritual life is to allow the beauty of God to shine forth in the world. Whether through the creation of an artistic masterpiece or the living of a holy life, we are called to be bearers of the divine light, to allow Christ to be incarnate in us and through us. In this way, we become participants in the work of redemption, and cocreators with God in the building of His kingdom on earth.

*There are countless church musicians throughout the world who dutifully strive to serve their parishes and their bishops, often in challenging circumstances. They persevere through difficulties, sometimes seeing great fruit, other times seeing little. What would you say to encourage them, and indeed all who labor for the renewal and reform of the Church?*

We must remember the parable of the sower: "A sower went out to sow. And as he sowed, some seeds fell along the path, and the birds came and devoured them. Other seeds fell on rocky ground, where they had not much soil, and immediately they sprang up, since they had no depth of soil, but when the sun rose they were scorched; and since they had no root they withered away. Other seeds fell upon thorns, and the thorns grew up and choked them. Other seeds fell on good soil and brought forth grain, some a hundredfold, some sixty, some thirty. He who has ears, let him hear" (Mt 13:3–9). We are called to be like that sower, generously scattering the seed of faith, beauty, truth, and goodness wherever we go. We cannot control the soil on which it falls, nor can we predict the harvest. But our task is to sow, faithfully and persistently. And whenever we feel discouraged and despondent, we must bring those feelings to prayer. Christ Himself experienced the pain and fear of the cross He was to bear followed by the abandonment by His chosen disciples. On Good Friday, as He hung upon the cross in agony, it seemed as though the powers of darkness had triumphed and His work had been in vain. And yet, that was not the end of the story. Christ offered all of His sufferings to the Father, and rose again, triumphant over sin and death, and confirmed His disciples in their faith and sent them throughout the world to preach His salvation.

*In this time of trial in the Church, I know there are many faithful priests, religious, and laity who feel as though they are living through a prolonged Good Friday. They see the Church they love suffering from wounds both internal and external, and they wonder when the dawn of Easter will break.*

As Pope Saint Paul VI describes, the building up of the Church requires diligent work and patient suffering. We cannot truly have the joy of the Resurrection without bearing the cross:

> To build the Church one must work hard, one must suffer. This conclusion upsets certain erroneous conceptions of Christian life, when it is presented under the aspect of ease, indeed of comfort and temporal and personal interest, while it must always bear the sign of the cross imprinted on its face: the sign of the sacrifice endured, indeed made out of love; for the love of Christ and God, and for the love of neighbor, near or far. This is not a pessimistic view of Christianity; it is a realistic vision, especially with regard to its construction, to its affirmation as a Church. The Church must be a strong people, a people of courageous witnesses, a people who know how to suffer for their faith and for its spread in the world: in silence, gratuitously, and always out of love.[3]

Whatever pain and sufferings we experience, we must remember as Christians that Good Friday is not the end of our story. With Christ, the victory over sin and death is already won, and like Saint Paul we can rejoice in our sufferings, for through them we are "complet[ing] what is lacking in Christ's afflictions for the sake of his body, that is, the church" (Col 1:24).

Christ gave the Church the mission to "Go therefore and make disciples of all nations, baptizing them in the name

[3] Paul VI, General Audience (September 1, 1976).

of the Father and of the Son and of the Holy Spirit" (Mt 28:19); and despite the sufferings and persecution we all experience, "he who endures to the end will be saved" (Mt 24:13). Our task, then, is to be faithful to Christ, to the Church He founded, and to the Scriptures He gave us—to "hold to the traditions which you were taught" (2 Thess 2:15) and to allow them to shape our entire lives. Christ began His ministry by teaching, and it is essential that we, too, hold fast to His teaching, which is preserved in the true and holy teaching of the Church today. For true teaching has the power to transform us, ever conforming us to the will of God. Today, we are scandalized by the sins and failures of the clergy, by the abuse of the innocent, and by the false prophets who preach a different gospel. The light of Christ, which should shine forth in our teaching and our witness, is obscured. But why has it come to this? Saint Paul warns us that we will inevitably fall into sin and error when we hold on to our former selves: "Put off the old man that belongs to your former manner of life and is corrupt through deceitful lusts, and be renewed in the spirit of your minds, and put on the new man, created after the likeness of God in true righteousness and holiness" (Eph 4:22–24). In all of this, through bearing either the sufferings of others or the sufferings that we create for ourselves, we must keep our eyes fixed firmly on Christ, who teaches us to bear the cross with patience, love, and hope. The crucifix must be our constant point of reference, and through sharing our sufferings with Christ, we too will share His joy in the Resurrection.

## *The "Program" of Holiness*

*Readers may wonder what sort of practical program or plan we are offering in response to the challenges facing the Church today. We have indeed made various suggestions, such as the restoration of chant-*

*ing the Divine Office, fostering vocations, supporting musicians and artists, and reviving the basic Gregorian chants outlined in* Jubilate Deo. *But in the end, the true "program" of the Christian life is not just a matter of specific initiatives or particular reforms, is it?*

The Church, indeed, is like the Prodigal Son, who, having wandered far from the law of his father's house, is humbled and contrite and returns home. God, the father in the parable, is always ready to embrace us, to welcome us back into His family. When the child left home, the father did not force him to stay. He respected his freedom. But when he saw his child coming back, he ran to him and embraced him. This is the heart of the Gospel: not that we are perfect, but that we are loved, that we are true sons and daughters of God who is ready to embrace us at every turn. Our vocation as Christians, then, is to become like Christ, to "put on the new man" of holiness. There are no shortcuts on this path, no "new ways" to follow Christ, as Christ Himself said, "I am the way, and the truth, and the life" (Jn 14:6). And in this life, the way of holiness is the way of the cross, of bearing our suffering and self-giving love and interior joy. It is the way that Christ walked before us and the way He invites us—to take up our crosses and follow Him.

For the errors and faithlessness that beset the Church, the remedy is to return to the sources of our faith, to drink deeply from the wells of Scripture and Tradition. If we immerse ourselves in the truth of God's Word, if we allow it to penetrate our hearts and minds, then it will gradually transform our lives and indeed the whole Church. We will begin to think and act in accordance with God's will, and the light of Christ will shine forth in us more brightly. For we must remember that in the end, it is God who will build His Church, not we and our meager efforts. All that we have and all that we are comes from God. The faith we profess, the sacraments we celebrate, the Tradition we have inherited—all of these are gifts from the Lord, entrusted to us to cherish and to pass on. We do not invent a new faith, a new Tradition for each generation, but rather, we receive it humbly and gratefully, allowing it to shape our lives and our worship.

In the midst of our earthly trials and sufferings, we must remember that we are pilgrims on the way to the New Jerusalem, the holy city where God Himself will be our light and where we will see Him face-to-face (see Rev 21:23; 22:4). As we celebrate the sacred mysteries here on earth, we are already caught up in the eternal worship of heaven. The Eucharist, in particular, is a foretaste of the heavenly banquet, where we will be fully united with Christ and with one another in the perfect communion of love. May this reality inspire us to live each moment in the presence of God, offering ourselves as a living sacrifice of praise (see Rom 12:1), until we too can join our voices to the eternal song of heaven, face-to-face with the one who is Love itself. This vision of the heavenly liturgy should fill us with hope and longing, even as we strive to make present the beauty and truth of God's love in the valley of tears that is the world. Christ invites us to share in His great and salvific work, to be His co-workers in the vineyard. May we respond to this call generously and with faith, giving our lives in service of the Gospel and in witness to the unfailing love of God. And as we labor in the Lord's vineyard, we must keep our eyes fixed on the ultimate goal of our journey: the heavenly liturgy, where we will join the choirs of angels and saints around the throne of heaven in singing the eternal hymn of praise, the song of Moses and the song of the Lamb (see Rev 15:3).